THE
POWER
OF
MESS

For Sofiyah, Amelie & Kika: just in case this is my last, and because you always have a way of making the mess magical.

And to the Great Mess itself: there's a song in you I am still trying to find each time. Sometimes my heart hears it; sometimes it doesn't. And that's why I wrote this book. All power to you and onwards into the music . . .

S.C.LOURIE

THE POWER OF MESS

A guide to finding joy and resilience
when life feels chaotic

yellow
kite

First published in Great Britain in 2023 by Yellow Kite
An imprint of Hodder & Stoughton
An Hachette UK company

3

A CIP catalogue record for this title is available from the British Library

Trade Paperback ISBN 978 1 399 70925 5
eBook ISBN 978 1 399 70926 2

Typeset in Fournier by Hewer Text UK Ltd, Edinburgh
Printed and bound in Great Britain by Clays Ltd, Elcograf S.p.A.

Hodder & Stoughton policy is to use papers that are natural, renewable
and recyclable products and made from wood grown in sustainable forests.
The logging and manufacturing processes are expected to conform
to the environmental regulations of the country of origin.

Yellow Kite
Hodder & Stoughton Ltd
Carmelite House
50 Victoria Embankment
London EC4Y 0DZ

www.yellowkitebooks.co.uk

Contents

Maybe we are not supposed to finish
our lives all tidy and pretty . . .
it's the messy hair, the bumps,
bruises, hobbling, wobbling, stutters,
rips and shattered glass pieces
that tell the story
of a thousand experiences.
That really tell we have been here,
that we gave it our absolute all.[1]

Preface

It's become clear to me over the years that the purpose of healing can be succinctly summarised as how to get our joy back. Of course, that's not what all healing is about. It's also about emotional integration, self-autonomy and how to learn to be present in this very moment, rather than lost somewhere in the past or in a future that might never arrive. It's about how to forgive life and ourselves and those who have hurt us along the way. It's about how to stick at this life when the storms come (or emerge from inside us). But how to bring back that sparkle in our eyes and that skip in our step is why we all begin the often arduous trail into the wilderness of healing. We want to feel what it's like to run towards life instead of trying to escape it. We want to learn how to look at ourselves in the mirror and not turn away in shame. Without getting our joy back, this life can so easily feel heavy, lacklustre and meaningless. But with a sense of joy, everything becomes possible, a lot of life becomes workable and the hardened edges of life are noticeably softened.

My most well-known poem exemplifies this passage of healing in a way that has spoken to thousands of people across the internet since my initial sharing of it:

I started calling that girl back . . .

The girl who loved living,

the girl who danced instead of walking.

The girl who had sunflowers for eyes

and fireworks in her soul.

I started playing music again,

hoping she would come out.

I started looking for beautiful moments to experience,

so she would feel safe enough

to show herself,

because I knew she was in there.

And she needed my kindness

and my effort to come

to the surface again.

People often write to me telling me how the poem has spoken to them
and significantly helped them on their own journey of healing. The
first question I am always asked is . . . what inspired the words? To
cut a long story short, the poem simply came out of an extensive
focus and period of time dedicated to opening my heart again, after
decades of both involuntarily and deliberately keeping most of it
closed. Because that's what a human being will do when we go
through difficult and overwhelming times (what I call the messiness
of life) and don't have the toolkit or support system to process those
events and our feelings about them. We shut down.

   It's an instinctive and automatic survival strategy and an attempt
to protect the most vulnerable parts of who we are. And we often
start to lean on this habit of 'shielding' ourselves in childhood, when
our mental and emotional faculties are most impressionable, still
developing and suddenly overwhelmed. It happens when we are

wholly dependent on our caregivers to protect and sustain us, and, still, we feel or are threatened and, worse, harmed. This doesn't just allude to overt abusive circumstances like physical and sexual abuse, but includes a spectrum of experiences, like high-stress family/ friend/school dynamics, the impact of divorce and family break- down, generational trauma, bullying or being the recipient of consist- ently unattuned, narcissistic or absent parenting methods. And it reaches into feeling belittled or unseen, and having your genuine worries and emotions patronised and not taken seriously by surround- ing adults. But the predicament of this involuntary and natural response is that when we first close off our hearts, it is often an all- encompassing action that we are not mature enough to filter through and manage. So, we don't just close off to one person or one circum- stance, but our entire organism is shut down to some degree. These subtle or not-so-subtle levels of shutdown then become our new normal, as does the shutdown response to difficult moments in general, until we forget that we have closed off in the first place and live as though this new normal has always been the way. Yet, our sense of self continues to deteriorate in this new normal because emotional shutdown on any level is not a healthy permanent mind- state to live from. Nothing life-giving can grow from this state of being. Instead, the opposite happens – everything starts to slowly shrink and wane. We feel more and more estranged from ourselves and life feels more and more blurred, as this sense of shutdown permeates through the entire soil of our lives. Our attitude and approach to ourselves becomes covertly toxic, at least until the toxic- ity spills out in our choices and behaviour – like when we tend to form addictions and yoke ourselves to self-destructive patterns or when we struggle and fail to form healthy and long-lasting relation- ships. Then our warped sense of self becomes plainer to see. We start to hide in the corners and shadows of life because the heart-shutdown distorts the way we see and think of ourselves and the world around us. Decades can go by, where we are simply trying our very best to manage life with what feels like a permanent closure of the heart to differing degrees, even if we may not define it as that.

Consequently, much of our subsequent lives are lived in the surface of experiences as we exist in the surface of ourselves. Given that we are phenomenal organisms of cosmic and primate proportions, living on the surface of things can still make for a colourful and interesting life to some degree. We can still function day to day. We can still laugh, smile and develop connections with others. We can still reach general milestones in the human experience. But the longing to live like we are free, to indeed open our hearts fully again and not feel subdued and distorted by the heavy hand of life, I believe runs deeper. And it keeps knocking on the other side of the doors that are locked shut inside us, to come out. That is joy in a nutshell. And it is never so buried away that it cannot be found when we yearn and look for it long enough. The feeling of joy is the feeling of opening the heart. Once we live with our hearts open, we can carve out meaningful experiences led by our joy, making it the supreme axis of our life that everything else rotates around.

That's why I wrote that poem. That's why I wanted to connect with what I called 'the girl inside' me. I wanted to remember life (and my life specifically) outside of the pain, the distrust and the triggers. I wanted to live with my heart wide open again. And, at the time, I was realising just how shut down I had been and for so long. I was weary of what the shutdown had made of my life, my significant relationships and the way I saw the world around me. I have written this book, not as a commentary about shutdown, but an exploration of opening up again. Because that's how I found my power. And that's where your power also waits for you.

Introduction

We all have mess: a messy desk, an untidy room, a cupboard, a shelf or a box we haven't sorted out for years. What does that say about us? What is in those dusty corners that we are hanging on to or keeping at bay? And then beyond the physical side of clutter, there is also life's emotional messiness.

To be clear, my current understanding and curiosity in life's messiness pivots around the many happenings in our personal lives that don't go to plan. Instead of life following your lead, it throws you curveball after curveball. As that old Yiddish proverb so succinctly puts it, 'We plan, God laughs.' It's kind of like the side of yourself you keep hidden away when meeting someone for the first time. The parts you keep at bay when wanting to impress in an interview or in a presentation or on a first date. It's the 'other side' of life, family, parenthood, relationships, having a career and running your life that we don't talk about, primarily out of embarrassment, discomfort, pain or, even worse, shame. To offer some examples:

- The other side of family might be dysfunctional dynamics and unresolved generational trauma.

- The other side of parenthood might be broken relationships with children or child loss.
- The other side of relationships might be break-ups, divorce or abuse.
- The other side of having a career might be the irreplaceable things you have lost along the way or the mental torment that keeps you up at night because of the demands, drive or insecurities you have about the work you do.
- The other side of running your life could be the mistakes you have made, the things you have failed in, the imposter syndrome you carry around with you, the impulses that drive you into imbalance, any depression and anxiety you have to constantly find a way to cope with, the cycles of people-pleasing you find yourself falling into, the habits and patterns you get stuck in so that you can avoid conflict and problems that really need facing, and so on.

These are some of the things you might spend years trying to steer clear of, placate or tone down. These are some of the experiences you try to keep your heart closed off to or go numb in reaction to, in order to minimise the pain they cause. A lot of the time, they are the things you really want to talk about because they are consuming your thoughts and eating you up every day. But you don't, because you reckon you will be negatively judged, misunderstood or belittled in some way. And, worse still, you might be exposed and rejected.

It might be the void you feel when your child leaves home or the unworthiness that swarms you when you are made redundant or are trying to hold on to your job. It might be the anxiety attacks that catch you unawares at every turn. Or the way in which you can't seem to get over your heartbreak and everyone around you has got bored of listening to you. It might be how much you hate looking at yourself in the mirror or that you feel incapable of being truly loved because your difficult childhood crushed and distorted the way you see and feel about yourself. It might be the disarray you now feel because of an accident that changed your life entirely, or it could be a lifelong illness that never relents from making your life difficult and you feel isolated because of it. It might be the regret and loneliness you feel after making a daring move to leave your old life behind and set up somewhere else. Maybe it's that you feel you are drowning in financial difficulties or that you are finding it almost impossible to integrate back into the world after losing someone you love.

Much of life hangs in what I call the 'other side' of living. These are the areas of our lives we are preoccupied with at night and, yet, we're never taught enough about these dominant aspects of human existence when growing up. Partly because of this lack of healthy exposure, we feel ill-equipped, embarrassed and quite helpless when we personally stumble upon these difficult, challenging grey areas. We often feel swallowed whole by them.

When the messiness of life has your existence in its grip, you will find that any ready-made answers you might have discovered from past experiences no longer offer as much insight in the present. Your present experience has outgrown the limits of your philosophies in the past. It's when life happens in ways you couldn't predict and you trip over time and time again because you didn't see the potholes coming up. You shrug your shoulders more; the words 'I just don't know' and 'I am not really sure anymore' tend to fall out of your mouth before you can lean on any automatic assertion of how life is, was or is meant to be. That is the heart of mess, really; when you are unhinged and shaken by unexpected feelings or experiences.

And yes, we've all been there. And it's a space of mind we will revisit again and again.

～

Life is messy, but the only way is through. Through the quicksand; through the hard lessons; through the distress; through the trauma; through the mess and the clutter.

～

But what if the process of 'sorting through' didn't have to feel as draining as it often does? What if there was an adaptable way of resolving life's mess that could set you upon a path of discovering deeper and truer versions of yourself? What if the mess that comes up along the way actually liberated you into living an integrated, wholesome, blossoming life?

In this book, I want to turn the idea of a chaotic life on its head and show you that life's messiness is not necessarily as problematic as you think, nor is it as antagonistic as it often feels. I want to demonstrate that, by reframing your approach, your experience of it can go through a metamorphosis and leave you with new wings and insight to create a life of your dreams. I will share how to find order and sequence in the chaotic and show how there is genius lurking in the messy.

FINDING THE MAGIC IN THE MESS

Sometimes we forget: we can't experience heaven on earth without earth being there in the first place. Earth in all its beauty *and* tragedy. Earth in all its glory *and* chaos. Earth in all its wild *and* cultivated terrain. We always assume the bliss is in heaven, but there is a kind of matchless bliss in the balance of the two, and the way they contrast and highlight the benefits and uniqueness of each. We rush through the finite to get to the infinite, not realising that the infinite experiences might be waiting for us in the finite also. We try to rush through the moments of darkness to get to the light, but maybe the light is waiting in the dark. We do our best to put out the fire, when the fire erupts to burn away the chains holding us down or back. We avoid the mess to try to get to the magic, but maybe the mess has a lot of magic that we tend to look past.

This has been my quest for over a decade now, because the darkness and messiness of life are not going anywhere in this world. Difficult times come and go like tidal waves and they are unwavering in turning up. How many days actually go to the plan you set out for them? Not many. How many times do you find yourself in shock at another hard thing that has come up out of nowhere? Often it feels like too many. Suffering is as much a part of the human experience as love (some might argue it is even more so), to the point that we find ourselves constantly directing our steps to avoid the unavoidable.

I remember when I got so tired of being on the run from and on the lookout for danger. It was when the speed of life's messiness hit at such a pace and with such force that I could simply avoid it no longer, nor could I avoid myself anymore. I slowly realised I was living in a subtle state of shutdown. Well, it was subtle until everything around me collapsed. Then it became really clear that I couldn't keep living this way. The collateral damage created was too severe. I had closed off from parts of myself many years before. And that kind of extreme disassociation only slowly bred a kind of hostility towards myself that was like a time bomb, and it had finally gone off, shattering everything I knew to be my life. I knew I had to make the journey within and start opening up all those locked doors in my heart, air out the rooms and get some sunlight and fresh air in. But it felt frightening, because all I had was the shattered pieces of my life left over by the hit. All I had was the mess. I didn't realise it at the beginning, but that was all I needed – along with a willingness to not turn away as I had done in the past, to not ignore or pretend or reject or try to escape.

∽

That's all we ever need – a willingness to do what
we can to stop turning away and shutting down.

∽

What I have learnt from my own struggles and setbacks is that so much of our living, through day to day, is spent either explaining away the messy parts of our lives or feeling ashamed or frightened of them and hiding them away. We cover up our shutdown. We pretend we don't turn away. Or, worse still, we become resentful of the results they produce. But there is more to acknowledge, honour and integrate about those messy pieces of our lives we lock away than we realise. In fact, I want to propose that those pieces make up a map of homecoming; a guide that can lead you to your own wild and unscathed brilliance and potential underneath all that is perhaps regarded as mere rubble and seeming devastation on top. The best of our lives begins at the point of choosing to accept the messiest parts of who we are and all we've been through. To trace their value and stop punishing them as catalysts of failure, doom and shame. Because that's when we start living like whole people, rather than just pockets of ourselves.

The more love and understanding we can show for ourselves, the more our hearts will open and the more empowered we become.

The messy areas of life itself actually have an intrinsic role in helping us to do this, because it's in the face of suffering and struggle that those parts of ourselves are most triggered. But if we are able to perceive and handle our reactions and triggers outside of our old ideas and ways of dealing with them, a beautiful opening of the heart and mind can take place. Emotional wounds stop feeling like black holes we must avoid sitting with at all costs for fear that we will be swallowed up in the pain of them forever. They instead offer a golden thread to follow, like a distant trail of stars in the velvet night sky, navigating us towards a more integrated understanding of ourselves. We need to go to the places inside us we try to escape from. This can become an adventure of sorts, depending on our approach and aim, and with all we gather from this valiant mission, we can then shape our experiences, past and new, with belief and purpose.

If there is magic waiting for you in the messy and difficult parts of your life and you have been unable to locate it up to now, it makes sense to try approaching it differently, to see if you can get any closer to it. I want to dare to suggest that you can and will locate any undetected magic in your difficult days if you do this. Hold the ideas and encouragement in these pages to your chest when your heartbeat starts to quicken, as you courageously step out of your familiar patterns and reactions, into a new adventure and way of seeing and meeting your life, especially the harder and darker parts. I am cheering and rooting for you all the way.

GET READY FOR AN ADVENTURE

Dear reader, what I want to propose to you is that there is an adventure ahead of you. Not a gruelling and punishing task, but a meaningful rite of passage that promises to leave you feeling reborn and illuminated by the end. In the past you would have identified it as a central point of suffering, defeat and burden for you. But, through the guidance in this book and the willingness in your heart, we are going to gradually focus in on other significant details belonging to this adventure that have been overlooked up to now. This shift in focus and approach promises to be epic and revolutionary.

It is the adventure of not turning away from the inevitable parts of life you have tried to stay clear of up to now. Like the internal noise you feel surfacing when you are on your own. Or the huge mountain of bills and correspondence you need to start wading through. Or feelings you have been carrying like a noose around your neck that you need to get off your chest. Or the habit you just can't kick because you rely on the way it numbs and distracts you. All these aspects of adulting, and more. And yes, you can turn them into an adventure! Because they can lead you to the treasures of the brightest and deepest parts of you. Because they can give you back pieces of yourself you thought you had lost forever. Because, if you can learn to love yourself through the hard and dark stuff, you are growing the kind of love that can never be taken from you.

It is the valiant task of opening your heart again and learning how to keep it open, so that you can source and utilise the creative force inside you to boldly walk forward into a life infused by your deepest dreams. It's how you make yourself available to the beautiful possibilities in moments that you have only felt threatened by or hesitant of up to now. Imagine a life where threats are minimal and your fear is contained to not dominate your daily experiences in the world. You can have that. You deserve that. And in order to experience that, we have to venture into what might feel like a hostile terrain of rocky challenges. We are venturing into your chaotic, muddled and beautiful life. The messy and chaotic parts. May you begin with your head held high.

∽

You are the hero of this adventure.

∽

HOW THE ADVENTURE WILL WORK

At the moment, you might be oblivious of your capability and potential, but as you venture deeper into the experience, your growing bravery will gradually transform your eyes, so that you can appreciate the power and magic you have inside *you*. Certainly, this adventure will require you to be courageous and it will ask you to keep going when you want to stop and turn back. This is key. But don't worry, because you have kept going in life up to now and your courage is part of why you are here, right now, reading this book. And there is even more courage inside you, waiting to be activated. Participating in this adventure will sweetly surprise you of your potential – wonderful ideas and a capacity you might never have associated with yourself up until now.

This adventure is about meeting the mess and facing the chaos, for the sake of your beautiful heart opening all the more, for the sake of experiencing yourself at your most powerful, at your most loving, at your most healed.

Part One will explore how we currently deal with life's messiness, why 'sorting through' the mess often feels so heavy and draining, and why fearing it and treating it as we would an enemy just isn't working.

Part Two will dive into the different approaches and effective tools to equip you as you set yourself on the path *through* messy times, rather than always trying to tiptoe *around* them. You will become skilful in using these approaches over time. And, through regular practice, eventually, you will have a fully fledged toolkit to rely on and equip you in times of difficulty.

Part Three explores the leap into the adventure itself – when the great showdown between you and the messiness of life takes place. All you have learnt has to be tailored to the environment you find yourself in, especially when you come up against spontaneous challenges you couldn't see approaching before. There are distinctive signposts to look out for, to keep you on the path and to keep your heart motivated. There are different insights to find and unique wisdom to apply that you can only uncover in the heart of an experience, rather than on the edges of it. And this final part of the book will look at that.

You *can* do this. You *can* face your mess, despite your heart feeling broken in this moment or your life feeling shattered. You *can* meet the hard stuff in your life and make your way through all of it, with your heart open, or at least opening by the end.

I will be your companion along the way. And I am going to offer you suggestions (alternative translations of the mess), stories and poems to encourage you in your adventure. Look out particularly for the journaling prompts at the end of each chapter. These 'Write It Out' sections combine the art form of journaling and free writing with a little soul work. Self-awareness is such a prominent part of healing and integration. It's the way to creating a life where you manage your complexities to weave a meaningful existence out of them. For all that you are learning about yourself as you muse over these questions and prompts, you are making essential steps towards a healed heart and an integrated life.

Wherever you are reading this, whether it is on the train going to work or late at night, tucked up in bed and it feels like we may just be the last two people on earth, I hope these prompts offer you a subtle, magical experience, where you find yourself breathing deeper and feeling more relaxed about who you are, why you are and where you are in your life right now. And more than embracing them, I hope my words guide you deeper into the truths you carry deep inside that you often feel you don't have the time, strength or support to relocate, release or live from.

I call journaling an art form because sometimes it can take time and practice to write from your heart about what's in your heart without inhibition. It is something we get better at the more we do it. So, there is no pressure to empty out all your heart in the rawest and most transparent way in your first attempts. You may be an experienced journaler and therefore go ahead and take the prompts or questions in any direction you want to go in. But keep an open mind and heart and don't take so seriously the highs and lows of the process of sharing your heart. It does get easier – any struggle is temporary – and it is extremely insightful and cathartic at every stage.

∾

Journaling is all about emptying and unravelling,
rather than philosophising or trying to prove yourself.

∾

In these exercises, you are not trying to find the 'right' answer, you are just trying to put words to the feelings you have, so that you can become more self-aware. It's probably best to keep a pen and notebook (or even one of my journals) close by as you make your way through these pages.

You *can* open your beautiful heart. You *can* find ways to keep your heart open. And facing the messiness of life is a surprisingly powerful and meaningful way to do it.

   This journey is for you. And it might just be as quietly revolutionary for you as it has been for me. I am grateful to have you. And I am honoured to walk alongside you awhile.

We are more.

We are more than the tragedies and the beauties that have got us to today.

We are more than the dreams that are guiding us to tomorrow.

We are more than our truths and our confusions.

We are more than our feats and our failings.

We are more than our demons and our angels.

We are more than our habits and our quirks.

We are more than our suffering and our healing.

We are more than our poetry and our art.

We are more than it all and that's why we can trust and soar and crawl and stop and start.

We can dance with our demons rather than fear them.

We can feel scared and yet not be controlled by our fear.

We can deconstruct and reconstruct.

We can swallow balls of fire as the night-time in our world falls.

We can stand tall in front of any mountain.

Yes, we can face it all.

We no longer need hush our souls anymore.

We no longer need edit ourselves. Hide from ourselves, locked in a cage.

We are more. We are more. We are more.

It's now time, more than ever, to wholly engage.[1]

PART ONE

The Approaches
That Don't Work

Before we work on new strategies to process and make passage through the difficult moments of life, let's look into how we currently process life's messiness and why these approaches aren't working. We'll also address why we spend years trying to escape the parts of us that we really need to access and, also, the parts of life we need to commit to and make passage through, rather than avoid.

These next chapters might feel heavy in parts, but don't be discouraged, and take your time to work through them. Sorting through the mess is often a draining process until we find another lens to look through. You will have an opportunity to catch your breath at the end of every chapter and feel through any thoughts that have been evoked. We are bringing everything to the surface so that we can go on an explorative treasure hunt and eventually locate the magic, the invaluable truths that wait in the most unlikely places to set you free into landscapes that will make your heart sing.

CHAPTER ONE

The Signs of
Emotional Shutdown

My grandmother died a couple of days before Halloween in 2014. Honestly speaking, it was a death I had been waiting on for about four years. That's when she really took a turn for the worse. That's when her heart closed so much that she looked more and more stone-like each time I visited her in the care home. It was difficult to witness her deterioration and her ongoing disappointment in her body and life in general. And yet I could see she didn't want to let go. She wasn't ready to die, although she became deeply embittered by the end, lost in her own world and constantly saying she wished she actually was dead.

She suffered with dementia in her last years of life and her coherency dramatically deteriorated over the last few months, as her past and present blended into one. Although this was a devastating addition to the decline in her morale on most days, it offered an unrehearsed and surprising gift in my last time spent with her. In her mind, she was 60 to 70 years younger and we were on a cruise ship. She was telling me of the singer she had a crush on. She recognised me but didn't know me as her granddaughter. And yet she was affectionate and open as I stroked her brow and giggled with her, looking deep into her eyes. It was such a delightful and healing surprise to see my grandmother as a young woman and something I could never have experienced any other way.

I felt I was seeing 'that girl' inside of her. I was enveloped in her joy for a fleeting moment, and it has stayed with me ever since. That joy and openness had been locked up in her heart for as long as I could remember. She was a remarkably strong woman, and she was extremely British. She was a survivor of World War Two, being held in a camp throughout it. A few years after her freedom, she lost her husband, mother and auntie in the same road crash along a French mountain that had her in and out of hospital for the next year. I have no doubt in my mind that she lived in a level of emotional shutdown from that point on. So many poems she never dared to write through her life; so many stories she vowed to not share; so many spaces inside herself she promised she would never visit again, for fear of the indescribable pain, the wordless grief. I think she reckoned she would never make it out again if she did, and I understand that.

That moment on the cruise ship where time between us blended and blurred was two weeks before her death. It was one of the most beautiful times I got to share with her. It came out of the blue and now it floats in the ocean of my heart forever. I spoke at her funeral and burst into tears as I told the story of our last discourse together and, although I had been waiting for her to come to the end of her suffering for several years, her actual death impacted on me greatly. It was as though I was finally allowed to let her go. The process didn't happen overnight. It took a few months. But I could finally express the feelings I had felt for all those years – the loss, the missing, the affection, the longing to get some time back with her again. I could finally allow myself to fully feel these emotions rather than play numb and just get on with life. I had a handful of dreams about her in this time and one particular one really stands out.

WHY SHUTDOWN IS VALID

In this particular dream, she was happy and playful, much like how she had been the last time we spoke. She was captivating in how she carried herself, how comfortable she now seemed, talking about her life with distinctive wholesome awareness. And she laughed. She made me laugh. It was always the other way around when she was alive. She couldn't tell jokes, but she found nearly everything about our lives hilarious. It was always warming to see her laugh. And now she was laughing and joking, with a wicked sense of humour.

Quite randomly, she wanted me to know that physical touch meant so much in our world and was one of the most powerful gifts we had. And she missed it a lot. She missed the sensation of feeling her body on another, feeling the heartbeat of her loved ones on her own chest, feeling even her own pulse, the drum of life resounding through her. She missed how she could feel her heart break, both because she loved so hard and stopped herself from loving like she wanted, in order to protect herself. But even more than all the emotional feelings, she missed the physical sense. Touching a smooth kitchen counter or holding flowers in her hands. Feeling grass or sand beneath her bare feet or the way the tide would splash against her ankles. And even more than that, she missed the physicalised connection to life in all these things the most. She missed that subtle and physical sense of belonging.

She told me to hold my girls as much as I could, to cuddle them, to rest my cheek on their cheek (as my grandmother and I always did when we kissed each other hello and goodbye). To never get too busy for a good squeeze; to never get so lost in the day that I forget to look into their eyes and hold their little fingers and simply stop. Stop and feel it all and let them feel and touch me. Inhale the beauty and exhale the nonsense. She told me to breathe them in like there was no other day to get something like that done. She said they were the best moments, and not having such moments now was what she missed the most, being where she was, in this new chapter of her eternal story.

There was something so bittersweet in what she was communicating to me. It reminded me of the calm, unassuming and transient beauty of crepuscular rays peeking through the gaps in clouds on a soft, grey afternoon. Her face was soft. She carried nothing on her back. She was excited about this new chapter. And there it was – a gentle irony. There she was, looking over to me and reminding me that I was fortunate where I was, that I still got to explore life in ways she gently missed, even though it was me who missed her.

I always feel a little healthy shame when retelling this dream, because it's like a small wake-up call to me too. I feel like I could heed her words better. But I have been thinking about that dream, in a new light, since writing this book and it makes so much more sense in the framework of life's messiness, heart shutdowns and the power we activate in ourselves once we start finding the courage to open our hearts again – and keep them open, when in the past we would automatically seal them shut again.

I always thought my grandmother was telling me to literally touch more, to make better use of that sense and explore it. On one level, she was. She was telling me to see more too. To listen in more, to slow down, to not miss the beauty in the simple moments that always form the foundation of our lives. But, more than this, I think she was imploring me to keep my heart open to life. To not shut down for good, on any level, or at least try as hard as I could, because in the end, when you look back on your life's journey, it just won't be worth it.

When the chaos of life struck my grandmother, it was at such speed, and with such force, that the task of repairing the collateral damage it left behind naturally seemed insurmountable. The mountain was too high to climb. And so, in turning away from the mountain, she shut herself off from where the mountain climb might take her. She took a detour, which still gave her a wonderful life in some ways. But she shut down considerable parts of herself forever, in the wake of destruction, to prevent having to holistically experience that kind of brutal shattering again.

My grandmother married again. She continued living. She showcased that uncanny durability of the human spirit to survive the harshest conditions, but the trauma of her extreme experiences yanked her away from some of her deepest longings and imaginings. Her experience of war and the loss of her close family members meant that she locked pieces of herself away forever. She was warning me not to do the same. Not in guilt. Not in shame. Not in fear, resentment or bitterness. But simply in love. And perhaps in hope too, because she knew, more than most, how difficult it could be.

I understand why she coped how she did. I haven't yet been through that kind of heartache and that degree of loss. And, quite frankly, I hope I never will. I am not sure I would be as graceful and gracious as she was in the years after those events. And simply surviving some tragedies is a marvel in itself. But I think we can all relate to that kind of reaction in most of the harsh moments we've personally endured. We've all shut down in the face of break-ups, falling out with friends and family members, betrayal, failure, job loss, and just the general wear and tear of trying to live in a complicated world that you feel misunderstood and invisible in. Turning away and shutting down are common responses to life in most degrees of human suffering, not just the most extreme circumstances of it.

WHEN SHUTDOWN BECOMES DAMAGING

Shutting down was the way I dealt with my childhood trauma. Indeed, it's the routine way of dealing with any kind of trauma. Running away from myself and avoiding my flaws was the way I handled all my internal issues (from childhood) that started to rear their ugly head through my twenties. I hadn't been shown another way. It was frightening and initially overwhelming to feel. Nobody teaches us how to deal with pain, so numbing myself towards my issues felt like the only way to manage them.

But when you shut down, you turn away. And yet whatever it is that causes you to shut down subtly continues to dictate the choices you make and the vision of life you have. Turning away makes you inaccessible to intimacy and those moments of vulnerability that the messiness of life can draw out of you. We fear that being vulnerable will make us weak, but in feeling stretched, overwhelmed and broken, you are actually pulled closer to *breaking open* and breaking through all those rooms inside your heart where you feel pieces of you are crammed into, lost or locked up in. In challenging times, because of having more to deal with than usual, you often don't have the capacity, the energy or the time to entertain all the masks, the worries and the thought cycles that would normally hold you prisoner and cloud your judgement, so your vision can become remarkably lucid. You go through surges of growth, because of the vulnerability you feel when your guard is down. These are the moments that can make you feel transcendental and firmly enchanted and inquisitive about this life here on earth. These are the moments that transform, heal and propel you outside of your self-created borders. And this works out to be the medicine you need to break out of the walls you have built to protect yourself in the past.

Unless we change how we approach life's messiness, in the first instance of seeing it, we close up shop. We tense up. We resign ourselves to struggling and barely surviving. We enter into a mind-set that can't note the openings, the deeper lessons and the brighter possibilities blanketed by the mess. And we turn away from ourselves, from our possible growth and all that we can learn about who we are.

Shutting down for a time in the face of distress is entirely instinctive. It's a protective necessity at times, especially in the immediate aftermath of upheaval, when we're locating the way through it and away from it, trying to get to safety. It's a medium to ensure the essential recalibration for our nervous systems to safely resume effective functioning, in good time. But it's when we make life-changing choices from the position of being shut down that the shutdown becomes a point of detriment, and an entry point for secret rooms inside of our hearts to slowly decay.

This is when the messiness of life in general becomes even more foreboding. Because we assign the automatic shutdown and flawed long-term choices we make to life's messiness, we feel even more threatened and untrusting of difficult moments when they show up. When we face future setbacks, the experience is compounded by the past memories and unprocessed emotions of feeling beaten down by similar encounters. We remember how much we have lost in past exchanges with the messiness and so, in the present instance, we freeze or run away and hide in the shadows of life all the more.

We collect and stuff the memories in a hole, deep inside us. We tend to stop embracing opportunities and possibilities, because of the small chance that we could get hurt and fall on our face if we do. Or we change pivotal aspects and expressions of who we are, or who we want to be, for fear that it could expose us to some kind of heartbreak down the line. We refuse to change, to mature and evolve and sometimes soften our philosophical insights because, essentially, we are scared to let more of life in. We are scared to give up that control that has kept us safe, although enclosed, for many years. This is when shutdown becomes undeniably damaging – when your heart-closure gets in the way of making the changes and choices at different points along the path that promise to be beneficial for your life overall.

Signs to look out for when trying to locate the damage of your own emotional shutdown vary, but it is important to look out for them and the specific ways the emotional shutdown shows up in you, so that you can better understand, manage and eventually heal from it. Generally, the damage can show up in:

- depression and anxiety (paralysing social anxiety included)
- being unable to locate and articulate your deeper feelings
- excessive people-pleasing, indulgence and spiritual or emotional bypassing
- overworking, overachieving and underachieving
- backing away from meaningful relationships, connections and opportunities
- finding it difficult to commit to things (relationships, hobbies, jobs and developing skills)
- adopting a cynical lens in daily situations, like always expecting the worst or being unreasonably disagreeable or defensive
- suffering with a racing mind and hypervigilance

- feeling randomly or methodically mistrustful
- having a strong inner critic

And there's more. Heart shutdown is something we are all working with and through to some degree.

Life is messy and curveballs will be thrown as surely as the ocean has waves. Just as it is better to surf the waves than be hurled about by them, it also makes sense to learn how best to score with the curveballs that are propelled our way.

∽

To not learn how to walk boldly and thoughtfully along the bumpiness of life's turns eventually does a disservice to who we are and what we are capable of.

∽

What if the mess is more a metaphor for our potential than confirmation of our lack of ability?

If you are like me, you might feel you have lived too many years of your life in shutdown and survival mode – and that you deserve more now. I can only echo that back to you. You *do* deserve more. You are worthy of a life led by your open heart, and the majority of your days exploring your deep joy, with a healed past behind you. There are fireworks in your soul to be set off again. There are sunflowers in your eyes to water. And you don't necessarily need to do it through any extreme measures. Because you can begin with what you have. You can begin by changing the relationship you have with the hard stuff in your life and refine your ideas around it so that the miracle of opening your heart once more can subsequently take place. Your heart is a work of art, whether it's open, slightly ajar or outright closed, but when it's open, and remains that way, it's an indisputable marvel.

Write it out

1. Which part of your life feels really messy right now and how do you tend to deal with it?
2. How would you define the messiness of life?
3. Write about a moment in your life when you found yourself closing off to life because of it. Have you managed to open up since? How did the shutdown impact on your life (consider both positive and negative effects)?

CHAPTER TWO

The Impact of Self-Blame

I remember another dream I had, years ago, where I spoke to a beautiful, old woman. She had many wrinkles carved deep into her skin, like the bark of a white birch tree, starved of water over countless months. Her eyes were softened by the decades of life she had lived, all the events she had witnessed, all the questions she couldn't answer and all those she could. Her grey hair seemed lit up with silver shimmers of moonlight. She was putting manure on the soil in her garden and the putrid smell was everywhere. Her hands were soiled with it. She laughed at me as I inwardly struggled with the idea of being enveloped by the waste of other creatures. She seemed to not have a care in the world. It was captivating. But I couldn't possibly open my mouth. I wished I was better at holding my breath.

'There is a lot of goodness in shit, once you get it out of your system,' she said candidly. I smiled. 'But it's the getting it out of your system that's the hard part.'

As she said that last sentence, I couldn't help but look at her fingernails that were velvet black with the waste. The dung was deep in, and it seemed a rather timely statement to make. I could only imagine how long she would eventually have to soak her own hands for. But here I was, in a strange, vast garden that had the air of the tropics about it, some leaves of the trees even bigger than me. I was in the presence of a fascinating old soul, being told about the value of a substance I gladly flush down the toilet every day.

Finding the 'goodness' within the waste, the toxins, the residue of difficult, core experiences is definitely the hardest part of the healing process. And in a small proportion of these experiences, it's impossible. And that's important to note. But those encounters with life where you feel an irreversible loss, where something precious from you has been snatched, when your heart has been broken into a thousand pieces, how do you find the goodness in them? The reality is that, through them, we form an aggressive dialogue with ourselves and the associated feelings that creates.

We use the 'shit' as reason to punish ourselves, to keep ourselves in check or in line and, more often than not, we do it without realising, through unconscious actions and cruel inner dialogue. In thinking we are doing the right thing and speaking to ourselves with mild or strong aggression, chasms appear in our inside world and our innate joy, peace, passion and aliveness get lost down them. So, we are often dealing with a double dosage of the shit in the first place. There's the shit that happens that we must first deal with – the sudden setback, an argument, some kind of disappointment – and then there's the shit we make from it and turn on ourselves through self-blame and self-sabotage . . . and that's the shit that gets into our systems. We regurgitate it in different ways, replaying the same scene over and over again in our heads, punishing ourselves, saying the same harmful things back to ourselves on repeat. And then there's how it affects our external worlds, relationships, opportunities, career paths, and so on.

For example, you have an argument with a friend. And you feel like you are being pushed into a corner, constantly being misunderstood and made to feel like you are solely the one in the wrong. Eventually, you lose your temper and you say some things you wouldn't normally say, in order to defend yourself from this 'attack'. The conflict leaves you feeling shocked, confused and manipulated. But because of your low self-esteem, you soon start echoing the untruths said about you to yourself, blaming yourself for the contention. You feel angry and guilty for trying to stand up for yourself. You replay the argument over and over again and you hate yourself for the things you said and the things you didn't say. That's dealing with a double dosage of the shit: there's the argument and then there's the way you punish yourself for how you dealt with the argument after.

Some of us have times in the month when we turn our frustration on ourselves the most, or we have triggers, certain events or happenings, words, energy or people, that are like catapults into this negative emotional activity. And this is a huge part of life's messiness. It's often when our inner and outer worlds are in contention with each other and we mask our true feelings. It's in this masking that terrifying isolation and estrangement can get a grip of our hearts. What the situation looks like on the outside contrasts greatly to how it feels on the inside and, because of that, we feel invisible, alien and expendable. For some of us it's when we look at ourselves in the mirror. Or when we don't say the things we want to say in what we think is the right way to say it. Or when our bodies don't do what we want them to – when they fall sick or unable or are over/underweight to some degree. Or when we can't let go, or when things aren't working out as quickly as they should, or when it feels like life is repeating itself again and again, so much so that we feel we can't breathe with the heightened feelings of mundane emptiness. Our frustrations become weapons we use against ourselves, when we find ourselves repeating mistakes, getting things wrong and when we feel life pointing out our personal shortcomings and weaknesses.

Up until my mid-thirties, my personal game of self-blame was at the end of the month. Each and every time, I was the loser and self-blame was the winner. It was the time when we needed more money than we had to pay our monthly bills – the rent, utilities, council tax, debts and the like. We never had enough money to run through to the end of the month smoothly. Life felt like it was just about stress, paying bills and dying. I felt like such a failure. Seemingly out of nowhere, I felt overwhelmingly incapable of living life, of doing what I thought everyone else was managing to do fairly well and especially at my age. I felt like a fake, like an imposter in my own life that I had passionately and sacrificially grafted for. It was anything from a few hours to a day or five (depending on the month) of relentless self-berating, scolding myself, mourning my mistakes of the past (that I thought had led me to this predicament) and wallowing in anger over my thinking when I was younger. I literally felt like shit. And I never felt so isolated and cut off from joy.

Throughout the month, I was doing my best to grow my life, to bring up my girls, to be true to my heart and my dreams. I was invigorated. My actions purposeful and conscious. I was taking risks and fleshing out a life following my intuition. But at the end of each month, when the bills consistently came knocking at my door, all the progress I was making became pointless. It was the biggest yo-yo in my life. I would feel content and at peace and define my life in the bigger picture for 25 days of the month, but in the last days, I would swiftly throw all that out of the window . . . automatically, without a second thought. Suddenly, I felt like I was lacking in so many areas of my life. And I was hostile and resentful towards myself. The shift was so overwhelming. I didn't take a moment to consider what it was

I was really saying to myself and to life. After it had passed, I would resume back to where I had been walking before all these feelings came up, near enough like nothing had happened. It was a cycle. It was a habit. It was my cage. There wasn't much else in my life that would make me feel so low, but this meant that my relationship with myself didn't feel like home, nor did it feel safe. This was the manure in my life.

TURNING IT INWARDS

One month, I had a little light-bulb moment as I was entering into my habitual thoughts about the end of the month. My innate fear of uselessness was rising fast, without apology or compassion. In a flash, I could see that my approach to fighting back from drowning in the intense and relentless stress of these moments was to get angry at myself – because at least with anger you feel a little less feeble. I directed the conflict within and used the tension as reason enough to put myself down; to in some peculiar way make myself feel like I was doing something useful about the practical problems I faced. In reacting like that, I was implying that being angry with myself was the solution to making more money, creating more opportunities, taking more risks and having the end of the month run smoother than it had been. Obviously, it wasn't. What I was really doing was using my anger and fear as a tool of mild yet effective self-sabotage.

What the old woman had said to me in my dream about getting it out of my system suddenly made sense. It's hard to get it out of our systems because we are constantly turning the 'shit' we experience in our lives back on ourselves, in different ways. Not only do we go through horrific ordeals and experience tragedies, rejection and abuse on an immense scale, but, at the deepest level, beyond our skin's surface and going right into our core, we blame ourselves at some point for these very things happening to us, or at least that is the kind of language, behaviour and feeling we participate in. It often feels like the only way to deal with the pain, the mistreatment, the shock. We don't know any other way.

By turning our pain and stress inwards, we are essentially blaming ourselves for the feelings we have. And life is rarely ever that simple. We have feelings within us not just because we, ourselves, have failed, but because we are deeply sentient beings, open, vulnerable and in connection with one another and all the brokenness we each carry every single day. Rather than turn our disappointments on ourselves as a form of unconscious punishment, better to understand our feelings, resolve them, heal them, be real about them and do so with intention, self-responsibility and structure.

Until we learn to do that, in a bid to regain some power and some sense of usefulness in the horrible experience, we turn the toxins in the feelings we have about these particular events on ourselves, through self-blame. It's our attempt to find our way back to the surface of the waters so we might escape drowning from the pain behind such encounters. Self-blame and taking responsibility for our lives are two very different concepts. Actually, self-blame is often a distorted attempt at trying to take responsibility for things. At the time, the self-blame feels like an inverted pursuit of empowerment, but really, we are stripping ourselves of our own inherent power and complicating the storyline we need to heal and move on from.

The problem with turning the obstacles and crises we are faced with on ourselves is that the 'shit' in them actually goes nowhere. It stays and recycles itself. It even grows. And with every exhale, we inhale it back in. So, the difficult event might be over, but because of how we use the residue against ourselves, those moments are very much alive in our bodies, our thoughts, our interpretations of the world and our perceptions of self. And they weigh and wear us down over time. They very much impact every way we read events, actions and moments in the present. No wonder when the messiness of life strikes, we feel so threatened and intimidated. We don't just see the mess – we see all the old shit, and we start ingesting it all over again. We need to stop making ourselves pay for the negative experiences we go through. Even the ones we solely or partly create.

∽

Self-punishment is never the answer.

∽

THE SHAME GAME

When a setback arises, another way in which we react is to feel ashamed. We assume chaos and difficulties have arrived because we have extensively and irreparably failed at something significant and, because of that, we are fundamentally failures. We feel angry and threatened. We feel guilty. We feel attacked. We feel low. We feel humiliated. We often carry all these feelings together. And, most significantly, the levels of shame that are triggered, the complexity of this particular feeling and impression, outstays its welcome the most. We have to get rid of this resident and regular overwhelm of shame in our lives, because it robs us every day.

Joy is a great healer, but shame will suffocate it. Love is a great healer, but shame will say we are not worthy of it. Peace is a great healer, but shame will eat up any bridge we build towards it. Perspective is a great healer, but shame will command us to keep our heads down, so that we deny ourselves, our opinions and beliefs opportunities to evolve. Life's messiness can also be a great healer, but shame will warp you into seeing it as an unforgiving form of punishment. It's when we lift our heads and take a small step forward that the sleeping magic within us is awakened, or at least made fertile once again. Shame is the biggest heart-closer there is. And I believe it to be the primary obstacle in developing a new approach to life's messiness.

It's really quite alarming when you start looking into how much shame the human heart can hold and the feelings of suffocating embarrassment that come with that heavy burden. There is an overload of shame and embarrassment hovering over most of us. Sometimes it will go to sleep, but, too much of the time, it is alive, awake and impacting the way we see ourselves and how we approach everything. It is the foundation of what I call the 'deficit mindset'.

This mindset is something we all suffer with to some degree. It rounds up the extent of unworthiness we battle with every day. It emerges when we solely define ourselves by the absences and losses in our hearts and lives. It is the viewpoint that predominantly focuses on and gets caught up in all we feel we do not possess or carry in ourselves right now. We get lost in all we have missed out on, in all the characteristics we wish we owned, in all the ways we imagine our lives would be different (and easier) right now if we had them. This becomes a vacuum in our lives into which all the good things also get swallowed up. It becomes a default perspective we readily lean on, so that, before we note what we have and own, we see and worry about all we think we are lacking. Over time, this makes us feel embarrassed, ashamed, insignificant and dispensable. And if these are the prevalent feelings circulating inside of you when life's messiness turns up on your doorstep, it's natural to feel alarmed and detrimentally ill-equipped.

Sometimes we are aware of the shame and the defeatism, but a lot of the time we are not, or only to a surface extent, because we are in the heart of it. It's difficult to see something you are in the middle of clearly and objectively. We are apologetic, inhibited, self-conscious, ashamed, powerless, frightened, anxious and self-reproachful, and we often feel like we are drowning in the challenges of life, past and present. All these feelings come under the banner of being consumed (quietly or loudly) by feelings of deficit, embarrassment and shame. The shame then continues to permeate from any sense of insufficiency we feel and this is why we will look at the world (and the mess) and feel entirely deficient.

We might be embarrassed of our jobs or the lack of money in our bank accounts. We might be embarrassed of our family history, our mistakes, our past, our failures, broken-down relationships, repetitive behavioural patterns and habits, our failed love life, the kind of person we have turned out to be, the way we look and instinctively behave. Or we might just carry a sense of unlocated shame on our shoulders, where we feel it but cannot place it. Our homes might be a regular mess. Our thought cycles might be chaotic. Our lives might feel muddled, always seeming less than what they 'should' be or less than the organised lives of those around us, because we can never seem to get a grip for one reason or another.

The point is that embarrassment is a universal feeling, and we feel it a lot more than we want to. *And maybe we feel it a lot more than we have to.* The fact that we feel subtly – or perhaps not so subtly – embarrassed about our lives and that we are not where we want to be, makes us often feel like a let-down, to society, to our families, to the way we think we are seen and judged and to the way we want to be seen. When you look up 'let down' in the thesaurus, an onslaught of words rush at you like bullets, if you are not ready for them:

disappointment, disillusionment, anti-climax, come-down, non-success, non-event, fiasco, setback, frustration, blow. This is the force of what we are faced with psychologically and emotionally when feeling in any way, shape or form that we are a let-down or an embarrassment to some extent. These feelings obviously can and do then creep up on us when we acknowledge our secret messes too – the messes in our minds and the chaos in our feelings. Often what we deem messy in our lives is therefore also a porthole for shame and self-reproach, disappointment and disillusionment.

When obstacles we face are distinguished and separated away from all our assumptions, narratives, thoughts and past battles of dealing with them, they appear dramatically differently. There are the challenges we face and then the stories we tell ourselves about those challenges. Life is hard enough. Life is messy. But it is harder and messier because of the opinions and recurring reactions we have about ourselves and our experiences as we face it. It is harder and messier because of how embarrassed and ashamed we feel about the disorder in our lives and about the past we are trying to leave behind. And it's necessary to note that I am not talking about the kind of healthy shame that enlightens you to correct mistakes you've made and grow and mature through the process. I am talking about toxic shame that grips your nervous system and makes you feel like you can never move on from anything – mistakes, trauma, disappointments, habits, and so on. It is the loop of learnt worthlessness.

The merciless and relentless internal belting of shame we tend to feel when things don't happen as they should is an integral cause for why we push ourselves so aggressively. It's why we are so scared to fail at something. It's why we don't take any chances. It's why we live unforgiving of our mishaps, mistakes and frustrating limitations. It's why we shut down. It's essentially why we don't like who we are and why we spend all our time trying to find peace with ourselves, outside of ourselves. And it's not peace we find, but short-lived ways to numb and subdue our inner demons from cackling in our ears. It's also why we can be difficult to live with and be around. It's why we might find it hard to apologise or why we can't stop ourselves from constantly apologising. It's why we feel like an imposter when good things come our way. It's why we doubt ourselves. I believe this is also a colossal reason for why we fear the messiness of life.

THE INNER CRITIC

The inner critic is the voice of the resident shame and unworthiness we carry inside, and it doesn't just eat away at the mistakes we make and the things we fail in. All the good we create for ourselves can also be perfect food that our insecurities are drawn to pull apart and devalue. If there is something to bite into, whether it's positive or negative in your life, the inner critic is not fussy, it will tear apart anything, until it is handled, managed and eventually subdued.

Through our lives we develop anxieties – a sense of disorientation in our own bodies – and we build walls and layers of stone around certain aspects of our hearts. And we have feelings about that; strong, unconscious feelings that build up a persona over time. It's a kind of residue that takes form. This form is the encapsulation of the thoughts that keep you up at night, the aches that keep you on edge through the day, the shame that weighs a ton and hangs from your neck so that you can't help but stoop. It's more than the shame you feel because that's what it feeds on.

This form is the culmination of the bitterness and hard-heartedness that grows inside us and creeps in unnoticed, often because we don't process our anger and hurt, unsure of how to deal with them, and so opt for suppression instead. Doing this over years, the feelings have to go somewhere and so they develop into cynicism, a sharp tongue, strong – and narrow-minded opinions, harsh judgements, compulsive behaviour, self-criticism, self-hate and hate of the 'other'. And there is no one more bearing the brunt of it, being victim to it and overwhelmed by it, than ourselves, as it controls the filter through which we look out into so much of the world, more and more as the years go on – until we start challenging it; actually, until we start starving it of the things it feeds on.

This residue left over from the harsh experiences of life is something we must face and work through. The messiness of life has a way of bringing up this residue to do just that. But the persona that has grown from it over the years will get in the way, internally intimidating and bullying us, and creating menacing narratives about the struggles and obstacles we face in a warped attempt to protect us from getting badly hurt again. We eventually give in and employ this voice that snubs us at any possible moment, in distorted efforts to try to gain some leverage with it. It's like a toxic parent–child relationship where the parent solely relies on screaming at the child and screaming down all their natural defences to curb their behaviour, so much so that the child starts to echo the words and aggression of the parent towards themselves.

The inner critic is all the justified feelings inside you gone sour and toxic. It is the encapsulation of being hard towards the world first so that the world can't be as hard back. It is your suffocated strength that has since turned to bitterness. It is the hurt and anger and distrust and hardness. It is the pain and self-harmful rebellion that hates any sign of weakness because it reckons vulnerability is an invitation to be attacked once again, by being used, neglected or ill-treated.

For every moment of innocence snatched from you, for all the things you were forced to see and feel, your inner critic grew. For every moment you were shut down and told your voice didn't count, it grew. For every slap in your heart that you stayed quiet about, it rose up. It rose in fury and it is like rock. It feels like nothing can break it down. Nothing can break it open. It is just something to survive.

It's a heavy burden to bear. We keep this undisclosed sense of dark feeling, different and more abrasive than sadness, at bay. But the constant presence of it subtly alarms us to what we're capable of, to what's inside of us. It can emerge as self-sabotage, as a sharp and spiteful tongue, as a short temper or strange and sometimes harmful impulses that we don't necessarily carry out. But it means we essentially don't feel good about ourselves at base level. There is something inside us that is impossible to trust because we don't actually know what it is, but it feels disturbing, and we fear it. It's why we feel so estranged from ourselves and so unsafe in our own skin.

We hide it as much as we can. We try to cover it over with a blanket of good deeds, meditations and healthy experiences. We wear masks and present ourselves in ways in which we feel we will be most accepted, hiding away our true selves because we develop such a low opinion of who we are when in the grip of this constant criticism. And we are petrified of rejection, also because of how it will fuel the inner critic. We deal with it alone like it is our cross to bear. We put our opinions on top of it as well as our beliefs, hoping to suffocate it. But it still remains, beneath it all. We are frightened of our loved ones coming too close and experiencing this sinister sense of personal distrust, this spitefulness that can just come out of nowhere when we feel threatened. We work really hard to reduce it. We inexplicably feel like bad people. The residue often articulates itself as self-mockery and put down. When we show goodwill, this voice in the background tells us we only do it to get attention or brownie points or sympathy. When we decide that today is going to be the day to make our dreams happen, we are cut down immediately with that mocking voice inside that scoffs at us for even attempting to change our lives, as though it is just better to accept our fate and watch everyone else be successful. It has a cruel opinion of everything.

A lot of us have ridiculously ferocious inner critics that are fuelled by the blame we allocate ourselves on a daily basis, stemming from survival strategies learnt from core past experiences. That's the fact. We have to get ourselves off the hook from this relentless, aggressive and blinkered way of treating ourselves. And how we automatically approach the messiness of life is actually key in this. When in the grip of the inner critic, we use the messiness as ammunition against ourselves. This also has the impact of strengthening the hold the inner critic has on us. We assume when the messiness of life comes that it is best to hide away and avoid it as much as possible so that we can better shield ourselves from the barrage of insults and negativity we automatically fire at our sense of self when the shit hits the fan. But once we get a handle on this and lean on a completely opposite way of facing life's mess, we actually edge ever closer to finding the keys that can unlock us from being bullied by the inner critic forever. We learn to starve it by pulling away from habits and reactions that fuel it. Yes, the messiness of life offers a ticket out of the inner-critic hell we all know so well.

GETTING THE SHIT OUT

Back to my dream about the old woman with dirty fingernails – and the realisation was luminously clear: I could never get the manure out of my system because I kept putting it back in me through the way I would habitually blame myself. And, without realising it, I was strengthening everything inside me that made me feel I couldn't trust myself – the shame, the deficit, the inner critic. When I felt stressed, I would personalise it. It obviously meant I was unable and weak, beyond the facade of trying to keep it all together. When I felt pressured, I would double it by telling myself there was no option for failure, giving myself a kind of ultimatum. Either I meet the pressure and succeed, or I would insult myself internally for hours, days and weeks, for not being able to do what I was supposed to do. I couldn't consciously remember a time when I didn't take my stress out on me. I would feel insubstantial and ashamed in my pain. I would feel annoyed at my confusion. My inner critic would have a field day.

∽

If you want to experience something different,
you need to do something different.

∽

I could lucidly see the web I was caught in. I was the spider who spun this web. I was the prey now captured in it. I could be the one to set myself free. I remembered the woman's words: *There was goodness to be found in this crap moment. There was value in my shit. There was something hopeful, compassionate and uplifting in all these details that had so far entrapped me.* I was going to take her word for it, rather than just repeat the same old habitual words and conduct.

I had to 'get the shit out'. If I got it out, then I could find whatever was good in it, if it was there. It wasn't a matter of mulling it over anymore. It was about acting in that very moment. The kind of psychological shame that makes you feel fundamentally unworthy, no matter what you do, I believe, is something we need to seek out tangible and *actionable* ways to remove. Because, if we don't, we will just suffer with no benefit in it for us at all. Suffering that is pointless truly is the worst suffering of all. As we'll see in the next chapter, if you can commit to pull away from the approaches towards life's messiness that don't work for you (or anyone) and never really have done, that liberating understanding – which will birth new and effective ways of dealing with the mess – will become your guide to a totally new experience with life's tough moments.

Write it out

1. What might be the manure in your life? What are the things that make you feel bad about yourself? And do you have any specific, recurring times when the manure comes up? (Maybe it's triggered by a relationship or a song or something else.)

2. How do you think you personally punish yourself? How might life look and feel if you found a way/ways to deal with the manure, rather than punish yourself through it?

3. Jot down a little of the kind of negative dialogue you regularly engage in with yourself when you feel triggered by something that brings up a lot of shame. Read it aloud. And then imagine these words being directed at someone you dearly love. Take a deep breath. Then write a letter to yourself to counter what you have written down, trying to broaden your view on your life and be more open-minded about the details. Rather than blame yourself, try to show yourself some grace. Try to be on your side. Remember the important details you forget when you get lost in self-criticism. Consider how this moment can propel you further. Look for a new angle and a new door to walk through in this familiar ground.

CHAPTER THREE

Making the Mess Your Teacher

I t is imperative to our potential – and to our joy – that we learn to grow out of the shame and embarrassment that are conjured up inside us when life doesn't go according to plan. When you can access your joy in the heart of messiness, it noticeably lightens the load and offers new ways of managing the difficulties so that you can remain open-hearted, access your power and watch yourself grow in the process. Shame distorts our perception, so it distorts our perspective, which, in the words of Viktor Frankl, is 'the last of the human freedoms'.[1] We need to be able to access and remould our perspective with the changing details of our lives if we are to open portals within the heart to find and birth something new for ourselves.

Understanding shame and embarrassment, guilt and fear, and becoming aware of how they strike and the events they emerged from, is a significant component in any journey of emotional healing. When difficulties arise and we find ourselves shrouded in these feelings, a lot of the time what we are dealing with is the residue of these unprocessed old wounds and experiences echoing through our bones and being, rather than any thorny challenges in the present moment.

Let me be plainly obvious here: getting to grips with our embarrassment is imperative to creating a meaningful existence, and I believe that one of the best ways to do this lies in approaching the mess of our lives in a new way.

I can imagine you already have a list of reasons why you don't consider yourself as a worthy contender to match the complexities of life's messiness with resolve and perseverance – even if you have done that to some extent in the past. Take a moment to consider some. Maybe you suffer and do your best to handle . . .

- unlocated yet paralysing self-doubt
- imposter syndrome
- a harsh and crippling self-critical voice inside you that makes you want to escape your skin when it's at its loudest
- childhood trauma or complicated relationships with your primary attachment figure and any of the disorders that come with that
- depression or a broken heart
- raging anxieties that makes you feel incapable and inadequate
- mistakes and setbacks from the past

All of these undesirable and complex components of the human experience have a way of defining you in your mind's eye. They are the buried shadows that emerge at the end of each day to haunt and tear at the meaningful, bright and stable parts of our existence, well into the night, when we are alone with our thoughts. We tend to secretly define our worth (or really our lack of worth) by the prattling of these darker dynamics that we carry around with us, which tend to control a lot of our significant choices and reactions. We look inside and, if we look for a certain length of time, it often becomes a painful experience, because we all carry a unique collection of these facets that we try to manage or at least survive the onslaught of on a daily basis. They in fact hang in the way of us being able to get a picture of who we really are. So, we distract ourselves and we seek out answers, strategies and fleeting comforts outside us, to keep these interior forces of thought and feeling contained. We keep our schedules busy with things to do so that we don't have time to look inside; we indulge in food, alcohol, drugs or sex; we follow after every 'expert' and seven-point programme that turns up on the scene. Then there's the people-pleasing, the over- or underachieving . . . the list goes on.

Could there come a day in the near future when we embrace the mess as a guide like we do the sun or the moon or some other kind of synchronised happening? Consider how useful a compass the mess in your life could be in this respect. Could this be a good enough reason to make friends with the very thing you once thought was your enemy and work together to overthrow the real nemesis, which is how toxic shame tends to ruin beautiful opportunities and moments in your life? As an example, say you are overwhelmed with the thought of doing a presentation at work. It's that unlocated shame that creeps up behind you and winds you out of nowhere. You struggle through the task, feeling unworthy and unable as you do and reciting how you will never be good at something like this. The process is indeed messy and almost torturous. You do the presentation. You hate every moment of it. You hang your head in shame afterwards and go home and indulge in pastries, biscuits and lots of fizzy drinks (OK, I am giving away my bad habits here!). You end the night feeling nauseous, unable to trace what you have in fact eaten because you were absent as you did, and you crawl under the covers, hoping that tomorrow doesn't come. But what if you could turn an experience like that around? And as soon as the task of the presentation lands on your lap and the shame creeps to the surface, you take it as sign that it is time to get to work on being kind, remaining open-hearted and refraining from engaging with the automatic discourse you would normally get into with yourself. What if you used the mess and how it makes you feel as a signal for how you need to support, nurture, empower and love yourself? This would completely change the game and give the mess in your life even more purpose.

Messiness is a foundational part of our human experience. We don't remove messiness from our lives; we get better at integrating it and befriending it so that it can guide us to phenomenal transformations of self and deeper comprehension and harmony with the ways of life.

TWO FUNDAMENTAL TRUTHS

Life's messiness is not the biggest obstacle to overcome in this journey. It is not the enemy. And neither are you. If there is any kind of enemy, then that title falls at the feet of shame. And the point of this adventure is not to get you in your best emotional shape to face and pass through any great threat looming over your head. It's more significant and valuable than that. This adventure is not about your strength, or even your courage. It's about your freedom.

But before you can set foot on this adventure, you need to first acknowledge or at least be willing to consider the truth in two certainties:

1. Life can be and is often difficult

This is an inescapable and obvious truth, but it's also perhaps one of the hardest things to accept about life. If someone asked me to broadly categorise the journey of life into two halves, I would be tempted to summarise life as the before and after of surrender to this fact, because of how significant the impact of that shift is. This is truly one of our biggest and constant struggles: to not feel immediately defensive when the difficulties of life strike because we either think they are wrong and unfair or that we are unfairly wronged by them. We deal with life being difficult over and over again. We tolerate it. We expect it even. But the multifarious degrees of disappointment we feel, and our efforts to avoid impending challenges at all costs, choosing instead to bury our head in the sand like human ostriches, discloses how much we grapple to accept this aspect of life. The expectations and longings we have for life to work out very differently from how it often does also gives away our strife with it. And yet, some of your most poignant experiences and openings of peace lie on the other side of interactions with life based on accepting and surrendering to this very fact – to stop trying to change what is essentially unchangeable. Life remains the difficult conundrum it often poses to be, but we can instead use our energy to make ourselves stronger, by learning to work with and alongside it, rather than protect ourselves in fear because of it.

2. The general challenges of life are more universal than they are personal

All of our life stories are categorically unique to us and so should they be – it confirms the brilliance that only you can showcase and explore in your life and why you are always irreplaceable and indispensable. But as you share your story and listen in to others, you will find there are common denominators, like definitive moments, events and exchanges in the human experience, that you can relate to and share common ground on. For example, we all know what it feels like to be rejected or have our hearts broken. We all know how relentless life can feel and what feeling overworked and stressed looks like. We will bring different specific details to the table, that make each of our stories unique, but our stories evolve around the same kind of central themes of looking for love, dealing with rejection, healing from neglect and unfulfilled needs, how to manage overwhelm and failure, not feeling enough and other facets that make up the human condition. This becomes better crystallised with age and there is something deeply reassuring about that recurring truth. Through it slowly integrating with your everyday responses to life around you, you start to not feel so on your own, isolated and facing all these odds that once felt like they were entirely against only you. That truth opens up a path for you to take your place as a *fellow* human being in the world as it unassumingly implies you are a part of something greater, older and wider than just yourself.

Once I started to accept these two truths, my comprehension of what difficult times really were went through a transformation. I started to look at my past hurts and present challenges outside of how I had always approached them. No longer were they isolated and random attacks that could strike again at any moment and were the cause of my corroding hypervigilance. They were confirmation that I was alive. They were proof I was like everyone else. Once I understood the fact that we are all dealing with different scales of struggle a lot of the time, I could then settle down to learn how to manage this pervasive part of life better. I stopped feeling so alone.

One of the harshest side effects of difficult times is how isolated and estranged you feel in trying to survive them. But if you can reframe them to create a bridge of solidarity between you and the world, that can soften the blows a hundred-fold. I am a firm believer that we have more in common than we don't.

THE POWER OF MESS

The power of mess doesn't lie in its appearance, in its devastation on your life or its contents. The power of mess is in the extraordinary opportunity it inadvertently creates for you to be set free from the chains of shame that hold you back from accessing your own power. What makes the mess so difficult on a personal level is that, to some degree, we are forced to face any pain and shame in our hearts that it brings up. What makes the mess a potential point of alchemy and personal revolution is that very same thing.

~

You have to learn to pull yourself away from beating yourself up over everything.

~

Once you reduce all that extra destructive dialogue that goes on inside the mind, you will feel better equipped to meet whatever obstacles are advancing towards you up ahead. This is how our relationship with life can transform.

This is something I have only really understood in recent years. I have realised that I have been a victim of shame's constant antics for decades. Conceding to a sense of general embarrassment over my life fuels relentless internal disapproval and condemnation (aka the inner critic) and deepens and strengthens the shame, making me *feel* more incompetent and unable to handle life. It's illuminating when you begin to acknowledge the way you take your own pain out on yourself.

Over the past decade I have committed to sever my attachment to this invisible act of constant self-destruction, especially when it became clear to me that the web of self-blame turns inward and feeds my inner critic. I am better at making space from the spinning, toxic thoughts so I can just watch them, rather than take part in them. I breathe. And I know, deep down in my heart, that I want to stop beating myself up and feeling like a failure when I get things wrong. I want to stop being cruel to myself. We all want this. We all want to free ourselves from the prison of self-criticism.

Most of us have been so hard on ourselves for most of our lives. There's a huge task before us to neutralise the energy from the negative thought patterns we have invested in over the years. But it is meaningful work, and the results are wonderfully empowering. Again, never shy away from the work you need to do on your heart so that your heart can feel more alive for it. Like the old saying goes, life is tough, but so are you. I am a firm believer that the incredible courage it takes to survive life is the same courage we need to turn life around.

∽

If you've survived life to now, you've done the hardest part.
You've proven you have it in you to turn your life around.

∽

This particular coping strategy of turning stress and other negative feelings against ourselves has travelled so deep into our unconscious that it occupies mostly all that space in our brains that allegedly controls up to 95 per cent of how we perceive and respond to the world every day.[2] It can therefore take a while to decipher what it is we are doing to ourselves and how we are doing it, because often we feel automatically justified in the way we treat ourselves. If we are failing at something, it makes sense to punish ourselves for it. If life is hard and we feel incapable of dealing with it, it makes sense to reprimand ourselves for the weakness showing up.

We need to explore why we react like we do and really grasp how it impacts our emotional well-being. These collapses or emotional landslides begin, like with everything, with tiny rips here and there. And often with holistic and long-term healing in our emotional worlds, it is more a matter of reducing and mending the little rips, one by one, rather than trying to deal with the enormous wound, isolated on its own, that the rips create over time.

Once you start unpacking your inner world, you realise how much of your automatic reactions are made up of guilt and shame, formed from something in the past. They have very little to do with the present day. You are still carrying heavy memories and feelings. Today's circumstances are detached from what happened yesterday and yet your automatic guilt and shame projects upon and warps today's possibilities to seem as something they are not. Whatever you think about this round of facing the mess in your life right now might have nothing to do with the definite details of the difficult scenario you are confronting or hiding from, and all to do with what you have been through in the past. This could be why you find yourself going around in circles in life, not finding the breakthroughs you are so desperate for. You are directing your energy and attention to the wrong aspects.

I have often found that when the messiness of life strikes, there is a new beginning or a new (deeper and more fulfilled) version of ourselves just around the corner. We also find it, not by trying to tiptoe around the mess, but by wading through it, with small, intentional, calm steps, much like the survival strategy needed to break out of quicksand. But this takes time and experience to really grasp.

Just for a moment, imagine the mess in your life as a classroom. In fact, try to see the mess as a metaphor or a bridge towards new learning and self-discovery. And then, if you are reading this in the privacy of your home, say this aloud and slowly:

> *The messy nature of living has always been a kind of classroom*
> *for me. A place to settle my bones and body into. Then I open my*
> *heart and mind so that I can be reborn through it, or at least a part*
> *of me can pass through a kind of transformation process. When*
> *the messiness of life strikes, there is a new beginning or a new*
> *(deeper and more fulfilled) version of myself just around*
> *the corner. I will find it, even if it takes time and experience to*
> *really grasp.*

Now, take a deep breath. Let the words marinate inside your mind even if they seem unreachable right now.

Because here's the thing: to open the magic, the wonder and the genius hiding underneath the mess (some of the tragedies, disappointments, hurts and losses), the shattered pieces of glass need to be carefully gathered up and embraced, so that your true story can emerge; a story that links your brilliance and your tragedies, your turmoil and your growth, the potholes and the portholes along your path. To do that you need to look at each piece, own each part of who you are, integrate the darkness with the light inside you. You basically have to stop running away from the messes and the spillages in your story. You have to reconsider how to approach those vast portions of your conscious and subconscious life that are uncomfortable to acknowledge, because in them wait more of the answers you seek and assume are to be found on the outside of you.

I am suggesting that the hard stuff we go through can develop into validating, significant experiences in which we can nurture our potential, break open the substance and depths of our hearts and surprise ourselves. Through the hard stuff, we can grow in boldness and clarity, moving away from the shadows and corners of merely existing, into a life fortified with intention and wholesome confidence. I am also suggesting that the hard stuff is calling us home and to find our joy, as much as anything else in our lives. Even in the heart of the wild jungles of adversity, there are portals to deeper self-discovery and autonomy. And if you find them, nothing will shut you down for good again. As we travel through those portals, we are offered unique opportunities to make peace with our lives and how they have unfolded. You can come out of these periods of intensity feeling more connected, present and synchronised with this mystery we call life. And you can feel more settled and confident in your own becoming. You just need to train your eye to find those very portals. And the only way to do that is to go meet the mess and face the chaos, rather than dodge them both and pretend they are not right up ahead in the middle of your path, waiting for some kind of interaction.

So how do we open our hearts?

HOW HONESTY OPENS THE HEART

The point at which to start emptying your heart is when life has turned upside down. I am not suggesting that chaos primarily comes our way in order that we get honest with ourselves, but confronting chaos in whatever form it comes does present that opportunity. And we do the best for ourselves when we take it. Getting honest is the first thing we should do when encountering life's messiness. And it's the second and the third thing, and indeed the last thing. Because being more straightforward in our internal and external dialogues creates a clearing for us to see ahead with lucid vision. It's a medium of powerful reassessment. It's a process of clarification that is more illuminating than anything else. It presents the initial way out of shutdown or inertia and into healing, self-discovery and self-actualisation. It's why therapy is so effective, because it teaches you how to be honest with yourself. And when we start speaking what we mean to say, our words become incredibly potent, creative and supportive of our deepest and purest intentions for our lives.

When you thought your life was going one way and then suddenly it's not, take it as a signal to check in and get honest with your thoughts and feelings. Imagine how a curious child would lift up a treasure box and empty it out until everything fell out; this is how we need to approach our own hearts. If we take this as an opportunity to do exactly that, to get curious and check in with all we are carrying inside, it is actually the beginning of life turning the right way up again. This is how you start to turn your life around, even in the heart of hard times. It's the way you stay afloat when tousled by raging seas.

I believe we can summarise our passage through life as the sum of creating, remoulding and finding again the pieces of the mosaic that makes up who and what we choose to be. And I have come to find that we leave pieces of who we are on the trail of our self-discovery and expression, all the way through life. In learning how to be honest with who we are and all that influences how we see ourselves, we edge ever closer to reuniting with these pieces of our puzzle, so that we can feel more whole. Like there is a trail outside of us that we can follow again to reunite with parts of ourselves, there is also a trail within us. And for most steps you take on this internal trail, as you empty and open your heart a little more, the emotional relief you find in making those steps is immense because, most times, you come across a piece of yourself you left behind or lost along the way. The reunion might be painful initially because the reasons we left them behind are painful. But it becomes a deeply invigorating and validating experience as we say the things we never got to say, as we give ourselves the space to see and feel through what we never wanted to see or were allowed to feel before.

> *It's not so much about how we sit with the pieces of ourselves we are proud of – that's easy to do. No, it's more about how we treat those pieces of ourselves that we don't feel so proud of. That is the space where the kindest magic can happen. The space where healing and wholesome living can occur and empowerment can be retrieved. Love those pieces, darling. Treat those pieces like the missing parts to the treasure map of uncovering the life of your deepest dreams. Because if we can love those once unlovable pieces, there is no longer anything that can stop us from blossoming into everything we are deep down.*

When we get honest with ourselves, we step into an understated but ever-present superpower. It doesn't matter how dark and heavy the memory lane we are walking down is. It doesn't matter if our honesty is full of sorrow, regret, confusion or resentment. The feelings evoked to the surface are temporary (even if you have been holding them in for years) and, as soon as we open up about them, they enter into a subtle and healing process of transmutation. Because, as we'll see in later chapters, a lot of the pain, self-estrangement and tension we carry is in keeping these feelings subdued and as hidden away as possible. Sometimes, just in coming clean about the ugly untruths we are yoked to, without beautifying them in any way, can feel like we are getting a huge weight off our backs and chests. The thoughts and feelings we have about everything are essentially temporary and are predisposed to adjust and transform. So, they cannot condemn us as we get honest about them in ways we often fear.

The point of honesty and awaking the power in it is this: we step into our vulnerability (the very thing the inner critic hates). We get beyond the masks, the beliefs and the coping mechanisms. We get through all the complexities, and the twists and turns in how we try to carry ourselves. And we step beyond all that too. That's important to note, because so much of our experience of ourselves is often caught up in those complexities and coping mechanisms. We are granted a sense of clarity that is incomparable, because our hearts are at their most naked, raw and open. We have put our defensive tendencies to one side. We have stopped editing ourselves. We can't do what we normally do to keep a lid on what we are feeling. And we have removed the walls we use (certain beliefs and opinions we have) that normally dictate how and what we see. We are able to use our faculties and energy to understand who is looking back at us in that mirror with what feels like new eyes.

There are two approaches that work effectively well together in the journey towards emotional healing and wholesomeness, much like how our lungs inhale oxygen and exhale carbon dioxide. The first is to learn to create new experiences that are based on what makes you feel alive (inhale your joy). We tend to undervalue the healing and spiritual properties in seeking out joy and pursuing experiences that offer back simple fun, like pursuing creative activities or going on adventures or trying out some kind of new pastime, because they are comparably uncomplicated. I would encourage you to do this alongside reading this book and throughout your healing journey. It offers a wonderful balance to the episodes of emotional intensity you will inevitably pass through when engaged in repairing your heart. The second is to replace your automatic shutdown reactions to difficult times, learnt from childhood, with an integrative process and perspective. Over the coming chapters, I want to focus on this approach, because it's generally harder to apply due to how deeply entrenched the impulse is. But some of the greatest encounters of joy are found on the other side of doing exactly that. Getting honest begins that process.

I want to suggest to you that it's not the details of the mess that are most important (although they are still entirely noteworthy), but the approach you take towards it, and then how you define yourself in the midst of it. That's when facing the mess and making passage through it can bestow you with insight and wisdom to help actualise the deepest and most loving wishes you have for yourself.

There will always be misfortune, disappointment, setbacks, mistakes and losses we have to deal with. But there are a series of ways for you to get out of the tendency to hold yourself back and shut off from life and all its possibilities, as an unintended consequence of trying to protect yourself from these difficult and messy aspects of living. You can experience a life of not feeling like you need to hide away in the corners of your world anymore.

There is nothing more powerful than an open heart. And there is nothing that proves strength and power more than the act of opening a heart which has been closed for a long while and then learning how to *keep* it open. Yes, I am a firm believer that you don't ever need a new heart, a different mind or personality, or even a new life. You just need to find ways to open what you have.

Whatever mess you are faced with at the moment, by the end of this book I hope you will know you can get through it. The lessons you learn in holding back from old protective habits can take you to some wonderful places, inside of you and around you. You will need courage to do this. But on the other side of your courage is the activation of a quiet strength and power inside you that will only keep growing and propelling you forward to all that is deeply meaningful to you, to all that really matters. It will be something you feel more and more proud of and excited by. And once you really merge with it, it can never be put to sleep again. Let's get going.

Write it out

1. Empty your heart onto the page: anything you are carrying; anything you feel you are dragging or is dragging you; everything you don't mention to the world around you; anything you try to avoid inside of you. Whatever comes to your mind, whatever circles inside of you, write it down and get it out in front of you. Do this first thing every day over the next few days and whenever else you feel drawn to do it in the day. Edit nothing; refrain from trying to find a neater more pleasing way to express yourself. Let's start making some space for this new adventure.

2. Once you have emptied yourself, take some quiet time just to sit with yourself. Write down the next things that come to mind. Write down the dialogue you have with yourself. Remember, no editing or trying to make things more pretty or wise than they come up as.

3. Consider what you honestly want for yourself in terms of this new adventure of dealing with life's messiness in new ways. How would you like to experience yourself in hard times? Envision it. Write down the details.

I want it to happen for you.
That day.
When you announce the great war is over.
You wave the white flag
from over the barricades
and you commit to making home in your body again.
You will take that last piece of bread
and break it over your past like confetti.
Announcing a return to deeper roots,
with a song inside you beginning
and sounding a lot like healing.
You are alive.
Spill your heart on the sponge pavements of joy
as you begin to wander again, because you can.
Because there is no bogeyman.
Because all detours have turned to sand.
And returning home to yourself was always the plan.
Nothing is recovered when at war.
Every soldier comes back empty.

And that's why we must end this.

No more battle crying. No more fighting.

To offer grace in the clenching and the tightening.

And then to breathe deep with a wide chest,

because life goes by like lightening.

I wish this for you.

Joyous breath. A particular kind of rising.

A life beyond surviving.

When you realise you were meant for more than war.[3]

PART TWO

Your Toolkit

Now we've explored how our current ways of dealing with life's messiness aren't working for us, this section introduces the different approaches and effective tools to equip you as you set off on the path *through* difficult times and messy landscapes. This is to prepare you for your actual departure into the wild and unfamiliar landscapes ahead, in such a way that the old patterns of intimidation don't have as much power over you, your perception and your resolve. And with any stress and tension that arises, you won't use it and hold it against yourself, but instead will learn to let it pass through you, so that you can feel a kind of fluidity through the landscapes of your heart, even in the face of seeming inertia. This is your adventure. Your chance to explore terrain you never believed you could without shutting down, and to find the kind of beautiful scenery you can only get to by embracing all of life (its messiness included).

The chapters that follow will explore strategies and thought processes that will expand and deepen your inner life, by strengthening your roots and nurturing your relationship with self. They are the truths and methods you can always rely on to refresh and restore you, on tough days and nights, in the gloomiest of forests and the emptiest of wastelands. They will remain a bridge to your ultimate vision and inspiration. They will keep your heart open. There is truly a more joyful, open and daring you on the other side of this stage. And all you need right now to begin is a willingness to step forward.

We can now get to work on replacing the automatic reactions and interpretations that hold you back with strategies that will have you healing and believing in yourself more and more. Carry these principles in your heart like you would carry water, food, clothing and weaponry in your backpack, because they will sustain you. They are gentle reminders that weave in and out of each other. Sometimes it's the gentle truths that enable us and pull us through the most. Imagine the message in each chapter to be like an article of provision to carry in your backpack on this adventure into the mess and more.

Before you begin this section, get ready to empty your backpack of the things that are becoming noticeably heavier to carry, whenever you pick it up. We use backpacks to aid us in our travels and, sometimes when we return, we forget to empty them. And so, with each trip, the backpack gets heavier and heavier, with old things that are less useful now than they were in the past. So, with each message from the chapters coming, if they resonate with you and you want to put them in your bag, be willing enough to look for something you already have in it (like old beliefs) and take it out of the backpack so you won't feel weighed down, trying to carry so much and to hold ideas that clash with one another. You will then give the new idea space to form and grow.

CHAPTER FOUR

Getting Out of the Shame Game

When challenges come up, they inadvertently expose our debilitating ideas about ourselves that can steal away hours, months, years, even decades. As we explored in Chapter 2, we are robbed of something beautiful and profound every day that shame dominates our thoughts and feelings about ourselves. So, if we can look at all, or at least some, of the aspects in our lives that trigger that sense of resident shame and embarrassment, and reframe them, we then reduce the time of being on the constant brunt of that shame and embarrassment. And eventually we can do the very opposite of living in a state of constantly being and feeling robbed.

Rather than live through our shame, we can grow a sense of unconditional worthiness in its place. We can walk around feeling invested in, endowed upon and nourished by life and make the most of living here on earth. Rather than feeling robbed by shame, we can feel safeguarded by worthiness. It's a lot easier to be civilised to ourselves when everything is going 'right' and we are ticking all the boxes. But we need to forge a consistent dialogue of compassion and fairness with our own hearts that persists through times of disappointment, mistakes and breakdown in order to really establish a strong sense of good emotional and mental health. The most effective time to develop this is when our feelings of shame are peaking. You guessed it: in the midst of feeling inferior, intimidated and overwhelmed – in the midst of running towards life's messiness.

∽

You deserve to live a shame-free life, in a shame-free body.

∽

THE NEW PERSPECTIVE

We need to find a new door to walk through when messy situations turn up. A door that won't lead us into repetitive and cyclical self-hate, but will challenge us enough to surrender to the healthy pressures and pains of maturation and propel us deeper into living out our essence. And the truth is that there is a new door available to walk through, in every messy circumstance. There is always a different angle to take. There are always more lucid, insightful and comprehensive descriptions of the scenery around you that can enhance your present vision. This then will impact directly on your feelings and thoughts, and therefore your lived experience in this very moment. As William Blake wrote, 'If the doors of perception were cleansed, everything would appear to man as it is, Infinite.'[1]

The doors of my own perception have been cleansed. I have come to understand, and practise in real time, the urgent need to walk away from the shame game I had been embroiled in for nearly all my waking life. I stopped holding the stress like a battering ram against the confidence I had been previously growing and I let it go. It became strikingly clear that I needed to start talking to myself with respect.

A new doorway had opened up in front of me, and a new perception of my life started to grow.

At first, it felt strange and a little cheesy, but, soon enough, I felt all my faculties wanting to run to my aid and help boost me through this point of momentous transition. It's like the more integrated parts of me understood what was on offer through this U-turn. I balanced out my inner criticism by bringing other significant factors into focus; central details I never usually paid attention to because I never wanted to let myself off the hook. Things I should have felt proud of, but was shy to lean on until it was clear I needed to (like the amount of effort I put into life and the roles I had). Objective details that disputed the untruth of feeling like an indiscriminate failure all the time (like remembering that I wasn't isolated in my struggles; most people find life hard, even those who seem far more successful and stronger than me). It is quite disconcerting to realise how much we can treat ourselves like the villain throughout most of our lives, when really those accusations are unfounded.

As I made my way through this transition, I was holding back a flood of engulfing criticism, like a dam would suppress floods. The old habits were at war with this new energy that had risen to the surface. I could feel the tension and the urge to tell myself off for letting life down again, but I decided to keep resisting it and water this new kind of dialogue. I started to explain to my inner critic the other factors that made the situation what it was, like I was talking to someone who wasn't in my mind or life. I breathed through the impulse to turn on myself and instead did the opposite.

I experienced the transformative potential in contextualising the challenges we face with objectivity, grace and integrative positivity. Not the kind of positivity that denies the complexity of our emotions, but the kind that offers a wider canvas for them to settle in, so they don't overwhelm the whole picture that they are just a part of. I also experienced the immediate benefits of getting on my own side. Either we learn to do this or we hold the whole world in contention, like it's against us.

Why do difficult situations have to be proof of how much we are failing and not an indication that we are ready to break out of old habits into something new and more fulfilling, and proof of our valour to even get to this point? The shame game is the first lens of distortion that we look through when life breaks out of the patterns we have grown accustomed to. And it's the first lens that needs to be corrected, so that you can see all the other important details and variables that make up this moment that you are not to blame for, and that you shouldn't feel ashamed about. It's the only way to wholly make peace with this reality we are in. This is how to begin the process of finding ever-deepening peace with the messiness of your life. This is how you maintain that peace when the answers are nowhere to be found and life *feels* like it's bombarding you with more and more impossible questions. This is how you don't drown, remain open or unlock your heart again. You use any shame that crops up to check in and learn about yourself without bullying yourself into some kind of agonising submission. And this principle is at its most useful when the grey doesn't disappear, and the flowers don't bloom, and the heart feels like it will never mend. Choosing to consciously do what you can to finally leave shame-filled reactions behind, in and out of these moments, is the lever to open the doors of your own perception. This is how we can best tend to our days as the portals of infinity they essentially are. Whether they are chaotic or indeed harmonised, the most important variable is the door you choose to walk through to meet them. The following chapters offer some of those doors you can walk through that will help you slowly eliminate any looming toxic shame, sometimes without even focusing on the shame itself.

YOU DESERVE TO FEEL WORTHY

Worthiness is shame's opposite. Replacing shame cycles with an intentional rite of passage towards worthiness is the essential transition to make for anyone who wants to exist through an integrated consciousness. It's the kind of durable and matured consciousness that is able to perceive the surrounding world outside of old, personal projections. Looking at the world, events and connections taking place in our lives through the lens of shame is just another projection. It gets in the way like any projection does. But with a sense of worthiness that is becoming a little more intrinsic by the day, your vision is cleansed that little bit more. As you learn to stop using setbacks and kinks in the path as a reason to punish yourself, you eventually start to see outside of the shadows of your past. And what a wonderful, new world you come into contact with. It's wonderful because it's new. And your idea of life beforehand steadily falls away. This is the real meaning of leaving your past behind. It's not trying to escape it or avoid it or just move to the other side of the country or world away from it. Because we carry it wherever we go, until we start to deal with how much we carry it.

So, what does worthiness really look like? Over the years, I have approached this concept from two quite dissimilar angles. And, therefore, my understanding of it has changed accordingly. Worthiness looks and feels different when you are trying to reach out to it, like it's something outside of yourself, than when you are focused on growing it from inside of you. When you are trying to reach towards it, like it is a point of development waiting for you in the distance, the way it forms is through positive results. The way it declines is through negative outcomes and feedback. It has an erratic growth pattern, and it never settles enough inside your heart to feel like it can be your new base, for your sense of self to thrive and deepen in.

When you are committed to growing a sense of worthiness from *inside* you, it is not predominantly impacted by the outside world. It is about your immersion in the experience of life itself and your intuitive sensibility that is awakened through that bond, rather than the results that bond creates. The results are an extra bonus or disadvantage, depending on how you look at it. But they are a small detail in the ingredients needed to grow an awareness of your intrinsic worth, from the inside out.

When your passage towards worthiness is initiated through who you are and where you are now, it is an energy that grows and shows up as you tend to your life as it is, with vigour and focus. You stop wanting to run away from obstacles. You stop wanting to be on the run from anything, full stop. And you start running towards these hurdles with resolve, in renewed commitment to your life. Because this is the best way to show yourself that you believe in who you are, or at least that you really want to. You come out of hiding. Out of the shadows that have kept you accustomed to the dark for far too long. You start to take responsibility for parts of your existence that have always felt frightening to integrate. But the fear doesn't hold you back anymore, even though it's still there.

There is a new energy that has your interest, that you want to nurture, that you want to give a real chance. You participate in the process of healing, gently but with intention, because you realise you are worthy of existing in a healed life, with a heart becoming fuller and more whole by the day. It takes work. It takes focus. It takes commitment, but out of a willingness to really grasp this concept of self-worthiness, you choose the rocky path of trusting your waking instincts, rather than old impulses and reactions, to become wholly responsible for your life. You try new things; you allow yourself to make mistakes. You approach the old stuff with new perspective, and the main thing is that you stop running and you stop hiding.

You come out of the shadows. You speak up. You listen. You meet your obligations. You soften. You toughen up. You meet the discomfort of being yourself in a world that will beat down on you for having your own mind. You pull away from the idea that everything is out to get you, because you are now growing your muscles in new ways, and that in itself offers new possibilities, more worthy of your focus. You are starting to believe you might surprise yourself. You develop your instincts, allowing yourself time and space to get things wrong, because in developing any new skill (and following your instincts is a definite skill), you are going to trip up over yourself a lot throughout. But the point is, you become present. You make yourself available to life. You take risks. You rise up. You embrace the challenges. You challenge yourself to see the same scenery, conversations, roles and relationships with new eyes. You become more rooted in your life. You take it in both of your hands and you promise to steward it with grace, with an open mind and a willingness to learn; shedding any old beliefs, stories and impulses that have been holding you back up to now.

The above almost reads like a visualisation. May it weave in your mind's eye different images of the possibilities inside you and over your head, and cause you to feel quietly excited and determined about your adventure. Because the truth is, taking responsibility for your life, for your healing, for your blossoming freedom, and becoming more responsible and steadfast through it, is essential to any long-lasting growth and it feeds the needs of self to a transformative degree. It is the trail to empowerment, the passageway to resilience and the channel to inner calm and stability. And this is where we are headed. So that when life's wobbles happen, they don't create the body waves they used to in former years. A sizeable portion of any healing journey happens when you take the road you have crafted for yourself in new directions, but still keep a hold of everything valuable in it that you are responsible for. It's about integrating, rather than isolating. There's only so much healing you can do on your own, in your own chambers of introspection. At some point, you have to leave your cave with what you have learnt and processed of your heart up to now and show it to the sun or rain that immediately greets you as you step outside. You move towards life, rather than retract. *That* is worthiness.

We often imagine a sense of worthiness as the ability to declare to the world around us that we deserve what we want and we won't settle until we get it. That we will live a life where we do whatever we want, when we want it. But this is a kind of pop-culture version of it. It's also a concept of worthiness we lean into as we grow up through our teens and early twenties. It is an attractive idea on the surface, but it disappoints in the long run, because worthiness isn't about how you get people to see you, nor is it about how they validate you. It's more intricate and not as self-conscious as that. It's actually more sophisticated and finely tuned. It is also more open-ended.

Genuine worthiness will first investigate and explore what we think we want and get to the bottom of why we want it so much. We will remain open-minded and open-hearted as we do. Worthiness instead says, 'I will find out what is best for me, and I will head in that direction, even if I presently don't want that very thing right now.' Because a lot of desires, just like feelings, are born out of temporary circumstances and often change with the wind.

Worthiness is when you make the transition to no longer be the kind of person you have to make excuses for, because you are too busy, plugged into life. Your life and growing energy now do the talking. Worthiness soon becomes tangible. It becomes a force, an experience with yourself, your growing intuition and trust in life, to get lost in. It is best grown primarily inside you, with the occasional happening in your outside world offering you validation here and there. But you don't need validation from outside of you like you once did. Actually, what you start to look for from the world is not so much praise and acknowledgement, but proof of your sacrifice, your contribution and your commitment in how it is making a difference.

Through the budding of worthiness in your heart, you are more willing to leave the familiar cycles of blame and guilt that distort how we approach each day. You move away from extremes. You grow in confidence enough to get really honest with yourself and see life as it is happening, rather than how you have believed it to happen or want it to happen, even now. A kind of trust is born, between you and life. You even start to trust the messy moments as well, because they will help you to see what's in the way of worthiness taking a deeper place in your heart and life. And you start to say yes, without hesitation, to all adventures, even the really difficult ones, like the one this book is based on. I hope this appealing vision of all that can be felt inside you when you start working on reducing your shame by embracing life's messiness is tempting and fuelling you to commit to this mission until the end.

To see messy moments through new eyes, the residual shame has to go through a process of alchemy and make room for worthiness. We want to just change the way we do things or just stop moments from happening, without realising that our instinctive reactions reveal deeper activity taking place in our consciousness that is calling for attention, love and integration. If you find yourself seizing up when the difficulties of life emerge, rather than just trying to get through them, avoid them or change them, take it as an indication that you feel unworthy of two things. The first is that you don't feel worthy enough to be the person who is capable of dealing with the mess in a skilful and efficient way. The second is that you feel you are not worthy of becoming the kinder, stronger, deeper, brighter version of yourself on the other side of passing through the difficulty. So, every time you find yourself freaking out about some hard moment you have to face, take it as an indication that you have an opportunity to find, feel and own more self-worthiness through this passage. Approach it as though your car was running out of petrol and the light came on to show you this.

A NEW LENS, A NEW WAY, A NEW NARRATIVE

A life freed of shame is a transformed life, a transformed perspective, a transformed approach to everything. Yes, a life freed of shame is a transformed standpoint towards the messiness of life too. You can start measuring your responses to the mess as an indication of how your sense of worthiness is growing or decreasing as you continue to move closer to the life and sense of being you want for yourself. In that way, the messiness of life is always a guide and offers a service to you to some degree.

∽

Once you start managing the shame, fear reduces also.

∽

You are only so fearful because of the low opinion you have of your-self. With a mindset of worthiness that you nurture in any given opportunity, you learn to let the world slowly open up for you in a new way. The messiness that strikes isn't so threatening because it doesn't feel like life is out to get you anymore. You can settle in this life because you are realising you are worthy of it and so you feel more able to get through the moments where mess visits. This takes years to firmly establish into the subsoil of your life, but a little consistent time given to this slow and sacred alchemy goes a long way. And your resilience is always growing. Just starting the process offers almost immediate benefit. Starting to turn away from the habitual pattern of blaming, shaming and discrediting yourself, even through just becoming aware of the patterns themselves, gradually creates a new platform to see your life from. A whole new narrative can begin and replace the one that decided that when anything or everything goes wrong, it's because essentially you are a failure and will always be one.

You begin to see that not every setback is a judgement or condemnation of you or the world. Not everything that spoils your plans is seeking to destroy you. Challenges don't show up to expose you and your weaknesses. The personal attack we often feel, on a subconscious level, when chaotic moments occur, incredibly reduces and the internal reactions that are struck up through them go quiet. We step out of the world of fight, freeze, fawn or flight into new landscapes of curiosity, trust, surrender and discovery, all through empowered participation.

With toxic shame slowly but surely on its way out of your life and its foothold waning a little every time you water thoughts and approaches grounded in worthiness (which include far more than positive affirmations), you are then better able to see what the messiness of life could be communicating outside of your projections. This is the beginning of a whole new relationship and dialogue with life itself. Maybe there is a much-needed message in the mess. 'Tools' that grow this sense of worthiness that informs everything with receptivity and openness look like:

- Giving your life a true and accurate context, rather than just blindly blaming yourself for everything.
- Setting healthy boundaries so that you stop running yourself into the ground and you protect yourself from toxic influences and energy.
- Exploring the aspects of life that make you feel good and inspired, and giving yourself permission to enjoy those aspects.
- Getting honest with yourself.
- Pursuing the things that make life feel meaningful and purposeful.
- Practising self-forgiveness.
- Stopping the people-pleasing and the chasing and being overrun by a fear of missing out. (Yes, slow down a little, so you can smell the flowers along the path you walk.)
- Speaking up when you need to. Learning to say yes and no when you mean it, rather than getting locked into things you don't want to do, energy you don't want to engage with and conversations you don't want to have.
- Letting people in. Letting people love you.
- Taking your life in your own hands and committing to being the sole guardian of it.

Most of the time, there is always something to learn from life's messiness. And it gets our attention and communicates the wisdom or knowledge we need in an inimitable way. Much like how the darkness reveals stars that the light cannot, chaos reveals what order is unable to. This makes more sense as your worthiness grows. Without those strong shame filters, you can plug into the very meaning of things. You can trace the purpose in all that is happening around you and inside you. You can locate the reason, the causes and the lesson.

The answers and guidance do not come together straight away. There are highs and lows like you would find when climbing mountainous land. You find yourself heading off course and you bring yourself back. You work through trial and error and learn where you need to let things go, so that you can find an easier route to travel. Sometimes this takes days, sometimes it takes months and even years, depending on what degree of difficulty, and especially tragedy, you are working with. But you have removed the biggest blockage in your vision, and even if you have just started the process of healing and recovery, you are so much more powerful and lucid for it.

Write it out

1. What has shame robbed you of so far? How do feelings of shame show up in your body, your choices and the language you use? Considering the backpack metaphor, what would you like to feel in those spaces instead if you could? What would it look like to replace the way any shame shows up in your life?

2. How do you personally run from life and how do you hide? Maybe you tend to get busy or the opposite, or you get focused on others around you or pull away from intimate relationships. If you felt you could deal with difficult circumstances and that they might guide you to your potential and be the catapult you need to leave old versions of yourself behind, how would you perceive them when you saw them coming up ahead of you? If the variable that changed was what you felt and knew about yourself, what kind of impact might that have on your management of the problem at hand?

3. Your concept of worthiness will change as you resolve habits of turning stress and blame on yourself. Write down what worthiness looks like to you now, and then in a few months do the same activity to see if it has changed at all. Can you remember how you perceived worthiness a decade or two ago? How has it changed over the years as you have committed to different practices? And now, draw up a plan of how you can practise more worthiness in your life.

CHAPTER FIVE

The Power in Our Perceptions

How we *perceive* 'mess' is how we will *exist* through it. It might become a matter of how to survive it or it might offer the surprise of finding new ways to soar and feel lighter than you did when first approaching it. But your experience with mess begins and ends with perception. And that's why you have more power than you realise.

The field of perception is always in your hands, no matter what others might say, or how your inner critic might mock you, or what you may feel your track record says about you, or even what you may be contending with right now. And this fact is something to be excited about! Because what it signifies is that, once you become aware of this truth, you effectively have the last word in all your dealings with life and you can then work out the best kinds of 'last word' you want for your life. I didn't comprehend even an inch of this until I entered my thirties. And this only came alive to me when every other approach I had tried to establish my life on had collapsed under the weight of the ever-expanding abyss growing inside me. It kept growing until I stopped running away from myself and running towards that abyss, sometimes with my hands over my eyes.

Although we might feel powerless in the face of disaster, how we look at the chaos and any devastation it creates, and then set out where we stand with it, is perhaps the only variable we actually have in our control.

And . . . That's all we need.

In his book, *Man's Search for Meaning*, Viktor Frankl, a Holocaust survivor and groundbreaking psychiatrist, wonderfully summarises this truth, with the life experience to confirm its relevance and power, when he writes: 'Everything can be taken from a man but one thing . . . to choose one's attitude in any given set of circumstances, to choose one's own way . . . When we are no longer able to change a situation, we are challenged to change ourselves.'[1]

All you ever need in the face of any disaster, setback or struggle is one element of the problem at hand to work with. That element can *always* be your perception. This is where your sense of the fundamental power you possess deep down can *always* grow and be activated. Normally, all or at least most of the other variables are out of your control anyway. And you are only a prisoner when your mind, viewpoints and vision are controlled by those variables.

Your perspective is possibly the most adaptable and responsive aspect of your internal make-up and it will change hundreds, if not thousands, of times through your life. And so it should. A cemented and brittle perspective is the beginning of creativity's death inside you. It's important to develop a seasoned, steadfast and measured perspective on life, but it's also important to always want to expand, to learn and grow from your roots that have been tried and tested over the years.

Your responses and behaviour have their role to play in how you interpret the world around you when in the face of something difficult. In fact, your responses are potential doorways for discovering your power and capability. How we perceive the messiness of life is most times a more important detail than the actual messiness itself. It's the embarrassment, judgement and fear of it that poses as the biggest obstacle in our way. And that is the giant that needs slaying, not the mess at all. That is the giant that manages to shut down our hearts time and time again. Realising the power in our perceptions is a path to walk so that we can develop resilience and realise we can be giants on the inside too.

RECONCEPTUALISATION

Reconceptualisation is a process of creating a new idea to replace old ideas that you have had surrounding a specific subject or object. It is the imaginative means of exploring new angles and points of view to fill out your vision and understanding of something. It prepares the way for problems to become challenges and obstacles to become opportunities. And this is just the beginning. All the heavy things we associate with the older notions of 'problems' and 'obstacles' are left by the wayside and replaced with the inspiration that is evoked from embracing 'challenges' and 'opportunities'. And it is a superpower once you learn how to use it. It clears the way for you to best approach an initially intimidating issue that would normally crush you in the process. Through this shift, you then come out realising how essentially powerful you are and have always been. It is our perception of life that has the unparalleled ability to crush or empower us. If we don't reconceptualise the losses and the messes we go through, we will always be victim to them. We will always feel like a reed blown about by the wind, not having a say on where it gets to land. There is a passage for us to make at the entrance of every troubled time in our lives which leads to integrating our experiences rather than being controlled by them. What if we can become taller, stronger and wiser because of the challenge or through dealing with it? I believe in most cases we can, and it begins with the process of reconceptualisation.

It's like the work you do when in therapy. What you are essentially working on is how to initiate this superpower of reconceptualisation. You empty out your heart, session by session, so that you can be heard and feel better understood, and through the process of sharing in a non-judgemental and insightful continued conversation, you are able to see elements of your life in a better-adjusted way. Nothing of your story has changed, but the way you see it has. And yet everything feels different because of that particular change. The possibilities for positive change have multiplied. The sense of freedom and peace is novel. This is indicative of how powerful perspective is. If we can learn how to lean on perspective and deepen it when we are desperate, we can always find the insight we need to navigate through the darkness, even if it might not be what we momentarily want or expect.

So as your mind thinks, so does it perceive and then respond (or react as the case may be). And then what often occurs after that is a perpetual cycle we get lost in. We continue to see around us what we are used to finding. But this cycle begins with how we read into our circumstances and the angle we take. Again, to draw on a commonly used metaphor, if you are surrounded by giants and you feel small in their presence, three things are most probably sure to continue:

1. You are likely to feel small and inferior in their presence (and probably away from them too).
2. You start to see giants everywhere.

3. You are then tormented by all the subsequent feelings and thoughts that stir up inside you, like unworthiness, helplessness, fear, self-disbelief and shame.

But if you were to reconceptualise your perspective with the suggestion that you too are a giant in the presence of other giants, then you might still see giants all around you, but (and here's the important part) they won't feel so superior to you and you won't be so intimidated. Imagine the kinds of thoughts, feelings, realisations and possibilities *that* angle on your life would conjure up instead. I know this is easier said than done, but once you get into the habit of learning how to lean on reconceptualisation to equip you with the clearest and boldest kind of insight and vision, you will be telling yourself this too. You will be the one in your corner, cheering yourself on as you dance with any giants in your life.

The 'Great Mess'

An effective reconceptualisation I still use to this day is one that is based on grouping the messy instances in life under one name: the 'Great Mess'. Rather than feel like you have to look over your head and dodge a thousand bullets (and possible enemies), it's effective to contain the challenges of life to just one part of it.

This Great Mess reconceptualisation has helped me develop a new relationship with different messy times as they swiftly approach my life, with the same velocity and seeming aggression as raging waves hitting the shore. I want to offer it to you now that you are aware of the old dynamics and framework of reactions towards difficulties when they arise, and can actively start the work of trying out new ideas and approaches. It's quite straightforward and refers to the growing respect I have learnt to show trying times over the years, essentially because of the possibilities for self-development and deeper life meaning they have offered. When the Great Mess approaches, I now try to advance towards it as an opportunity to learn about this one side of life. I used to cower away, especially because of its intimidating 'greatness', but by reducing my inherent levels of shame and growing my sense of worthiness through some of the approaches explored in the chapters ahead, what were once details to avoid are now usually invitations to expand and grow.

So, from this point on, if you are willing, and until you feel you can get nothing else from this book, I am asking you to commit to identifying any difficult road you are facing right now as the way in which the Great Mess is showing up in your life, right along with me. It's not the whole of life. It is just one part. So, rather than call it 'the worst break-up I have gone through' or 'the darkest time in my life', replace it with something that simply suggests the Great Mess is knocking on the door of your heart once again with yet another passage to make.

THE SUPERPOWER THAT REALLY WORKS

When I was 18, I saw something that would stain my heart with a subtle terror for many years to come. My then-boyfriend (now-husband) had returned to London the evening before, from being away in Europe for three months. We were sitting together at his aunt's house and, abruptly, he stood up and started twisting his neck. It looked like he was trying to do something impossible with it, to somehow get it around his shoulder. Suddenly, as if possessed by the ghost of an owl, he got up from the table and sat down with a dangling thump on the floor, now like a puppet, with his legs crossed. He continued looking behind him, twisting his body, until it could twist no more. My stomach turned too. I was flurried with racing thoughts, trying to work out the spectacle in front of me.

Embarrassed to admit it now, I felt annoyed as to why he would suddenly behave like that. It wasn't funny. I was caught unaware with this absurd physical movement, and I wanted to tell him off for frightening me like that. I sharply told him to stop, as he continued to contort his body. He didn't respond to me. His movement became more amplified as he spun around some more and, after the most haunting cry that will be forever lodged in my memory, he threw himself backwards, with another thud. His body started convulsing, eyes rolling back. He was having an epileptic fit.

Had we been alone together, I can't tell you what I would've done. It felt like something wicked had suddenly possessed him, lurking in the shadows, waiting for the right moment to pounce. Luckily, we were with family and friends, and they kept me calm as they did what was medically necessary under the circumstances. With my cheeks constantly tremoring and my heart in my mouth, too frightened to take a deep breath, we watched my guy slowly stop shaking like a drill and eventually come back to consciousness, totally dazed and bewildered by it all.

He hadn't had a fit since he was 10 years old. Obviously, it was something he had never thought to tell me because it isn't unusual for children to have one-off fits. But that day we began a journey that flung me deep into living life on a cliff edge, whenever something would trigger the memory of that moment. My husband had a relatively mild case of epilepsy, but he started having fits more regularly. And I started going through the dreadful horror of being there when most of them would happen (and worrying about him whenever I wasn't).

I felt like it brought such a heaviness into our lives, such a heaviness into my heart. I wanted to slay it, annihilate it. If he was late, my thoughts would turn to the epilepsy. If he was unhappy, my thoughts would turn to the epilepsy. It was such a pain in my eyes. It took me years to put my labels to one side and understand it for what became its sacred purpose in my husband's life. But there I was, always imagining the worst, because it was the natural thing to do. I was also getting slowly worn down from the imaginings.

However, my husband did something quite extraordinary with this continuing experience. In a gradual surrender to this messy moment in his life, he started approaching the different details in a new way, and he began turning what had been a disempowering story up to now into an empowering one. Down this unlikely road of self-discovery, he found connecting threads that suggested that the very thing I hated, and thought was out to destroy us, could become a helpful guide.

ᕲ

Reconceptualisation can revolutionise your thinking and put you directly on the path of pivotal, emotional healing.

ᕲ

He stopped treating the epilepsy like the threat to his life it very much felt like (and could be). Instead, he chose to integrate it like a compass to help analyse deeper issues that he now thinks his seizures were in relation to. He began exploring the intricate relationship between mind and body, and the results were illuminating.

He started employing the moments immediately before he would black out as a way to face incredible anxieties he carried, because they tended to surface in such heightened moments. Each time he felt a fit coming on, he focused on noticing the details occurring again, so he could better prepare himself. As he started to feel the mental overwhelm swooshing in, racing through his mind like electricity, he would anchor himself, breathe deeply and try to relax. Eventually, after many failed attempts, he would 'pass through' the chaotic noise and intense pressure pervading through his body, without his brain giving up. This was monumental, for us both. His eyes would become electric, like he'd been propelled into space for a few seconds. He'd call it an incredible ride. He was amazed he could pass through the tunnel of terror. If it upset me to see him like that, losing control in such a way really frightened him. He said it felt like squeezing himself through the tiniest space, with walls closing in on him on every side. But eventually he was able to bear it. After that, he looked to give his epilepsy a context. He realised the disorder was just an extreme way of his brain trying to look after his body, because the electrical currency going through his head and body was too overwhelming. He realised it was his brain trying, in a roundabout way, to preserve the organism.

Through that, a portal for him to locate deeper truths and presently unexplored emotions opened, as he looked to the metaphorical implications (if any) of his brain patterning. What might his epilepsy be teaching him? What might it be an amalgamation of? He began to reflect on his tendency to escape a lot of things in his life, including himself, his pain and his unresolved past. He eventually understood that his epilepsy was a strange and unconscious way of him shutting out the world for a few moments. He did that for many reasons: because of many memories; as a reaction to general overwhelm; to protect himself as best he knew how. Through looking at his epilepsy as a guide, rather than an enemy – as something to understand, rather than something to rid himself of – it opened new worlds for him to make peace with himself, to heal old wounds, to eventually embrace himself deeper. He was able to connect the dots that seemed in conflict with one another and on the surface had made him feel fragmented and estranged from himself for many years.

In this perception of his disorder, his fits were steering him so he could, at some point along the way, release himself from a lifetime of running away from pain. That thought was enough to keep him going, to keep him digging, often in the dark. In this way, that time in our lives was so incredibly illuminating and significant. And I am not saying that epilepsy occurs solely for the reasons that he uncovered, at all. I actually believe these findings were personal to his own experiences. We're all unique. We all have our own reasons for being the way we are. It was just fascinating to see what we could discover once we changed our feeling about this problem in our lives. Sure, it was scary. There were days when it felt like there was a fine line between madness and miracle. We were walking on a tight rope, taking chances and risks. It was emotional. We tripped up many times. But more often than not, if the things we give our time to are not scary to some kind of noteworthy degree, then they are probably not the most beneficial things for us to be giving our time to anyway. It's always scary when you leave behind what you think you know. Feeling fear can often be a sign of travelling a road set on a worthy and liberating cause.

I have come to understand we only want to destroy aspects of ourselves we don't understand. We only close our hearts because there are parts of us we don't feel equipped or supported enough to process. We are only hard on aspects of ourselves we don't understand. We are only ashamed of aspects of ourselves we don't understand. Without understanding, there is no real healing. Without reframing the problems in our lives to be opportunities to grow and learn from, the chances of gaining integrative understanding from them become rather slim. Which is why reconceptualising difficulties in your life against a different backdrop, purpose and intention is a true superpower.

REDISCOVER YOUR POWER

Rather than tell you about how transformational reconceptualisation is, I want to show you how it works in real life and that the principles behind it can revolutionise your experience of the Great Mess, however and whenever it might show up. I want you to feel more capable to move forward and through issues in your life. I have learnt that on the other side of meeting those challenges are your deepest dreams and the possibilities for them to be slowly fulfilled. When mountains show themselves, you will feel more ready to climb them if you can reframe the sight of them in such a way to suggest they might just reveal some incredible wonders along the way, wonders that you can't reach on your own, where you are positioned right now.

A sizeable proportion of what we deal with in any messy situation is the truths or untruths we tell ourselves about the difficulty at hand. Any turmoil we feel can be divided into what the objective reality causes and what elements of it our subjective observations are drawn to. It's our very thoughts about the mess that the battle takes place in, and our thoughts both direct and follow our approach and perspective. If we can finely tune these two elements – approach and perspective – they become the magic components to get us surfing on the waves of the messy seas, rather than feeling submerged and battered by them. Reframing the thought that 'this moment is going to drown me' to 'this moment is going to grow me' can transform the experience, sometimes immediately, without any other variable changing in the objective world outside of our subjective lens. This is good news. It affirms the potential of your own power, once you learn how to plug into it. And you connect with it each time you actively participate in the process of reconceptualising something that essentially intimidates you, through some kind of action or change in your approach. But like with any kind of skillset or superpower, we must give time to practise with it, so that we learn how to best utilise it. In the beginning stages, it often feels, as my husband described, that you are hemmed in on all sides and the walls continue to close in on you. But there is a way through, even if it's through the eye of the needle.

Reconceptualisation is the passage we all must make at nearly any given turn, to rediscover our power, our purpose, our voice and the deeper truth behind different happenings in our lives that are not so easy to dissect at the beginning. Because we often approach them with a distorted vision. It is a revolutionary yet underrated tool we can always access. It is underrated because it does require a certain kind of stamina, and it needs to be committed to like a discipline until it feels more natural. It is underrated, until we are desperate enough to want to see our stories and lives with new eyes, because we are clear like the light of day that our old stories have nothing of goodness for us anymore. Churning them out over and over again is only holding us back. It is underrated because we tend to so heavily identify with our scarcely investigated opinions and beliefs about things. But it is like a dormant superpower that is yours forever and, once it becomes active, it propels you towards the most authentic aspects of yourself. I will continue to reference this point throughout the book because it is so vital to any genuine healing journey. It is an essential tool to carry in your backpack of wonders when launching into adventures where you will meet giants, monsters and, indeed, merciless mountains along the way.

Write it out

1. Is there anything you are going through right now that might be a guide in disguise?

2. How do you try to preserve your heart and mind when in the midst of overwhelm? Do you pull away? Do you distract yourself? It doesn't have to be anything good for you. Remember, my husband's brain would shut down for a few moments to preserve its organism. It often emerges in a misshapen form, but the intention behind it is there.

3. Write about someone you find brave and inspiring who was able to turn around a really difficult situation through approach and/or perspective.

CHAPTER SIX

Embrace Your Inner Storyteller

In my personal reconceptualisation, the Great Mess is not just a name, it has a character behind it, and I liken it to Roald Dahl's 'Big Friendly Giant' – scary-looking at first, intimidating, but soft-hearted in the centre and, deep down, only hoping for the best for you. By walking alongside it, and sometimes in the palm of its hand, you can gather some adventures, perspective and insight into your humanity you couldn't find without that kind of companionship. And although you fear you will be squashed or trapped by it forever, you never are.

Maybe the difficult moments in your life wake you up in the middle of the night and snatch your breath when you least expect it, much like Sophie experienced when first kidnapped in Dahl's beloved tale. Maybe you regularly struggle with something that makes you feel estranged and removed from any sense of belonging, or sense of safety and security in your own body, much like how Sophie might have felt as an orphan, essentially alone and hypervigilant in this world. If you decide to humour me enough and start calling your personal messy circumstances the 'Great Mess' too, feel free to come up with your own impression that makes the backstory more

relatable. We are now already in the process and power of reconceptualising, together. You might find the *BFG* story and character too
childish for you. You can be as creative as you want. And your visual
image can be made of squiggles or defined details. Just imagine in
your mind's eye some kind of giant, fearsome being or monster that
also possesses a softer side, that is hidden at first. The aim of the
reconceptualisation is to make any present emotional struggles:

- More tangible (which is why giving it human features helps it
  become more approachable and easier to communicate with).
- Less abstract (which is why we give it a fictional form and brief
  background, rather than just let it take up space and remain
  invisible and therefore immeasurable).
- Inclusive of your fundamental feelings about it (which is why it
  needs to be quite intimidating in some way). Otherwise, you are
  not being honest about the whole impression and are prone to
  falling into total denial about what you're facing. And denial is
  never helpful.
- Digestible enough so that aspects of it can surprise you in a positive way (which is why you want to create the image with a
  softer side). Through this, you are tapping into the broader and
  more complex picture of your life, rather than being solely tied
  and invested in the specific damning and mostly surface details
  at present.

I also want to ask you to imagine the Great Mess as a kind of
shapeshifter. It is full of its own kind of personality, but it might also
show up in your life as rocky and treacherous land to trudge through.
This is an exercise of the imagination, but the truth is, without your
imagination, however active and well-oiled it is or isn't, the process

of reconceptualisation is almost impossible to grasp. And our impressions of life remain narrow. Once we learn how to employ our imagination in this way, it can become such a creative and enabling force. We are in a constant process of subconsciously and consciously using our imagination all the time anyway. I am just suggesting that you be more intentional with it.

Reframing challenges is also a wonderful sphere to have some fun in. It is a kind of playground in the mind to explore. And to think that there is a filter that lightens the load when dealing with things that often feel relentless and cruel, is a surprising and precious gift. When it comes to the Great Mess, just imagine it in a way that encourages you to go forward.

∾

The key with the messiest aspects of life
is that they are not to be avoided.

∾

We are aiming to create a metaphorical depiction that is relatable and relevant, but less menacing. In this way, the difficulties you might be facing potentially become less detrimental to the stability of your life, especially your inner world because this directly changes your approach towards it. We are embellishing reality by adding giants, but remember the adventure of sorts you are on right now, through these pages. And actually consider how you approach difficult times anyway. Like you are incapable, smaller and naturally intimidated by them? That immediately sounds like how someone would feel when facing a giant.

The truth is, we are telling ourselves stories all the time, as we try to make sense of the world around us and inside us. And, even more than that, our lives are essentially a collection of all kinds of stories.

Some are entirely our own; others we have shared ownership of; and still others we have no hand in creating and still we feature in them. We can also be simple background characters in others, bystanders among the action we are sometimes directly impacted by. We all, deep down, want to be the hero of our own life story. And the hero either slays the giant or makes friends with it. With the Great Mess reconceptualisation, I hope you will consider as we go along that there is more benefit in the latter.

I can guarantee that you are already telling yourself a story about the messy parts of your life. Maybe you have told yourself that you are not worthy of anything better than the cards you have been dealt so far. Or that you should stop hoping for things to get better because they never will. Maybe you have decided that you will never be qualified enough to get a promotion. Or that all relationships are toxic, and you will do much better being on your own from now on. Maybe, deep down, you feel like you are really an awful person and everything is always your fault. Or maybe nothing is ever your fault. The point is, the stories we tell ourselves have a colossal impact on how we encounter each day. They create the framework for what we notice of our experiences and what we take from them. In the words of Michael Margolis: 'The stories we tell literally make the world. If you want to change the world, you need to change your story. This truth applies both to individuals and institutions.'[1]

So, for now, let us continue in this vein and imagine your life as the wider landscape in which the Great Mess has its territory. Yes, your life is bigger than the Great Mess. You can soar higher than its most elevated reach and your roots go deeper. Let us also envisage that the story of your life is not just any story, but a heroic one at that. And it is full of epic promise, in gentle parallel to Joseph Campbell's notable contribution to understanding the framework of the hero's quest in mythological tales, in his book, *The Hero with a Thousand Faces.*[2] Through his research on comparative mythology, Campbell illuminated the different stages in storytelling, of any heroic protagonist, who is set a challenge or adventure, which then catapults him into unknown territory, and forces him to face and consequently be transformed by unexpected disaster. This is a wonderful parallel for our own encounters with harsh circumstances and sudden challenging events. And if you like the thought of dealing with ogres, dragons and otherworldly elements along your journey, feel free to modernise these details. For example, the dragons of our day can be raging anxieties and stress levels, childhood trauma, inner demons, the longing to heal but not knowing where to start, pandemics, social media sensationalism, culture wars and real ones, nuclear threat, unpredictable inflation rates and fuel hikes. There's a lot of material you can work with that fits the bill!

But you, the valiant hero, waking to your innate courage a little more, every day, will come through this superlative adventure we call life, riding on the seas of love and loss and everything in between. You will experience the many twists and turns life is shaped with, in your own specific narrative arc. You will make friends with the most unlikely forms and beings and in the most unexpected places; joyfully surprising yourself as you do. You will learn how to make portholes out of potholes. You will get used to stepping up to any challenge, rather than backing down because of self-doubt. You will learn to stop yourself from overindulging in the flower fields of bliss so that you can preserve your balance and nurture your other senses.

You will grasp more and more that a certain level of struggle is required to create meaningful encounters. The experience of life will break your heart, but you will use it to break you open, and you will mend, countless times. It will astonish you again and again, not just for its direct beauty and wonder, but because even beneath the harshest of seas there are still beautiful worlds that are waiting to be discovered. And all of this is possible because you learnt to stop running away from the Great Mess and embraced your role as hero.

You started taking risks. You chose to keep moving forward despite the winds blowing against you. And now, as you are tossed by the aggressive waves and you find yourself in places previously unknown to you, it is there that the Great Mess will hold your hand. Because you have learnt to trust it enough to guide you into these worlds of meaningful experience. And you will fall in love with who you are becoming. You will learn to appreciate who you were, because we can never fully understand who we were without a newer experience of ourselves for comparison. And you will be saturated with peace in this moment, because you can freely look behind you and ahead of you now, without feeling you are lacking.

Imagine what life would look like if you borrowed the above suggestion as the new framework for the story of your existence and the context for all the hard things you are going through. Imagine if that was what you told yourself every day. Imagine how your heart might open. Imagine how ready your heart would be to embrace the joyful moments as they came up on the way through this journey. It's a reconceptualisation of your experiences. It's a statement of faith in who you are. And it is heroic. But what's even more heroic is actually considering that this could become the *concrete* details of your very life.

What generally works so well with using an epic genre narrative to pinpoint and shape your experiences is that it cultivates a gentle sense of deference and *purpose* to your every step, with a growing regard for potentially transformative landscapes you will come across. It encourages the best attitude and perspective inside of you to the surface, to assist you as you approach these life-changing challenges and trials. Naming these pivotal encounters or chapters in our life stories offers a growing sense of thoughtful sacredness that defines our experiences with value and worth, rather than just simply feeling like a calamitous collection of pointless suffering. Defining yourself with worth and value becomes easier once you can appreciate the experiences in your life in such a way; when you can put a sense of worth to all the tough moments too. As you find more worth, inside you and in your life, the courage you need to go in the direction of your dreams will only grow. And so will your resilience and, with that, a profound sense of safety will emerge from your heart. Because the resilience you develop will be the force to get you through the difficult terrains over and over again. Your life is never more epic than when you are your own witness to your courage accelerating in growth and how it transforms the surface and depths of your existence. Facing the Great Mess in your life showcases and strengthens your bravery like nothing else. This is why we have to continue to find ways to keep our hearts open or to prise them open when they seize shut.

GETTING OFF THE MAP

I have a long history of following everyone else's map but my own. I always refer to myself as a recovering self-forgetter, which is also known as a recovering people-pleaser. When I lost myself in one map, I would move on to somebody else's. I look back on those years, or at least the moments in them consumed by that intention, as the emptiest of my life. My exterior life didn't actually appear so messy. Everything almost worked like clockwork. I had the grades. I had the achievements. I was on the expected path to make everyone proud. But my interior world was full to the brim with silent screaming. These were the years when I lied to myself the most. When I wore the most amount of masks. I don't blame myself for it. I was young. I was going to follow whatever was put in front of me, but to feel alien in your skin because you are obsessing about how others will see you and treat you (if you can manage to get life right in their eyes) is perhaps one of the most devastating ways to exist in this world. It's only a matter of time before you rebel, regress or wake up. I only started considering the possibility of going my own way and drawing my own map in the wake of great loss.

∽

It is in reckonings with loss that we can be woken up the most and are compelled to break away from those inauthentic maps in life we're mindlessly following.

∽

The day you break free of the map made for you and start creating one for yourself, whether it's with a scream or a whisper, with a burst of energy to propel you or the drained capacity to barely drag yourself forward one inch at a time, you begin the rocky trail of creating a life on your own terms. It's both frightening and essential, both challenging and exhilarating. And it's messy, because the road is no longer linear, straightforward or predictable. It is no longer a copy of something else. It is curvy, bumpy and wild. You are working it out as you go along. Everywhere is uncharted territory. Better to be on a messy and muddled map that you can call your own, than on a tried-and-tested map that was born out of another's life and is slowly suffocating your own sense of identity.

I liken the roads we carve out for ourselves to the rocky pilgrim-
ages and rites of passage you find in mythical tales and folklore. They
masterfully combine the drudgery in making your way through harsh
terrain, against the backdrop of bewitching and rousing scenery,
while encountering all sorts of extraordinary 'creatures' and challenges here and there. With each encounter, with these ghouls, giants,
elves, faeries and more, we are further equipped, awakened to our
potential and more discerning of the twists and turns of life.

But, why does a passage that could be so potentially empowering
for us seem so foreboding that we will often stay on the maps we
know, deep down, we don't belong on, the paths that essentially keep
us feeling dissatisfied and trapped until something forces our hand, so
that we feel we have no choice but to start carving out a different
passage? The force of intimidation is something to be reckoned with.

We tend to immediately turn away from a tunnel of pitch-black darkness up ahead or when it starts to emerge from inside us. We pull away
from moments where it's unmistakeably clear that where we are going
to end up is unclear. The idea of tripping over ourselves, falling flat on
our face regularly and making mistakes turns us away so that we hide in
the corners of our lives rather than confront anything coming up ahead,
face on. You might think these instinctive responses are obvious and
natural. And they are. Nobody likes pitch-black tunnels. But our dislike
for these things is compounded not just by a natural dislike for such
circumstances, because of what they infer and demand, or because we
look out at them through the filter of deep unprocessed emotions we
carry within our hearts. We are also repelled to step further and forward
or to plunge inside because we haven't learnt yet how to make our imagination work for us. It's through the process of imagining what we want
for our lives and how we want to walk through and with life (and then
acting on those imaginings) that we begin to draw our own map.

MAKING YOUR IMAGINATION WORK FOR YOU

This component in our mind functions both like a dormant super-power and an intrusive lodger until we get to grips with it. We are always using our imagination. We are either imagining solutions or extensions to our problems. In our planning, we are imagining. In our hiding, we are imagining. In our doing, we are imagining. In our listening. In our resisting. In our expressing. In our learning. And, of course, in our dreaming. I am not necessarily talking about the land-scapes of our imagination that only the greatest storytellers seem to stumble upon and pull us towards. Any kind of active engagement, whether it's positive, neutral or negative, requires imaginative thought, a stirring up of visual suggestions.

For example, if you ask yourself right now why you feel so appre-hensive about your life, or the coming week, or a certain occasion or event coming up, it is perhaps because you think you'll suffer in some way, or it might be emotionally painful or something is bound to go wrong . . . You are currently imagining. If I ask you why you feel overwhelmed and disconnected, I am sure your heart might break out into the saddest song, and the reasons will revolve around not feeling good enough and feeling small and incapable and so on. You are imagining these ideas about you. You are engaging with a resident vision you have of yourself, which you may or may not be able to verify, but it is directly impacting on how you feel about yourself, your life and whatever the task at hand may be.

A recurring vision I have of my own self that has predominantly informed my feelings and default responses to challenges over the years – to a detrimental and paralysing level – is 'I can't do this.' I spend so much time thinking about how I can't do something and, yet, time after time, year after year, there I am, while imagining that I can't and won't be able to do a certain something, doing the very thing I have told myself I can't do. I met that vision of myself hundreds of times while writing this book. There I was, writing late into the night when my family was finally asleep, struggling to find the right words and how to streamline the message I wanted to come off the pages, while coincidingly imagining and struggling with the vision of me not completing the project.

We often get more and more disenchanted with each episode of chaos we are dealt as proof of our inherent inability. We see the mess coming up along the horizon and we sigh in disbelief, daunted by the intimidating, distant noises. 'Not again' or 'I can't do this again', we whisper under our breath, automatically falling into the position of the vanquished. I believe this happens more because we are entrenched in disempowering stories and imaginings than because of a factual prognosis of any menace waiting for us when life suddenly becomes volatile.

We imagine all sorts of things. And there is a direct and strong impact from our imaginings on how we move through anything. If we can become skilful in managing this area of our minds, it has the potential to become one of the most empowering facets of our being. It can become an incredible tool to enable us to move through the hardest circumstances with our hearts either open wide or slowly opening up again, so that we can access our joy when we need it most. We are often so much more powerful than we realise. But once we become aware of our potential, the horizon widens under the golden sun.

So, what if we imagined something else?

Write it out

1. Look out into the landscape of your adventure (your messy or not so messy life) and craft out the scenic details of it. You could even draw out a map that shows the different areas of your life and the passages you are making in each one of them, through the different scenery. For example, one area of life might feel more like rocky mountains or ominous, dark forests or mysterious rivers, home to elusive creatures. Be as creative as you want. But the setting is important in any work of reframing, because we instinctively and immediately respond to our environment. So, flesh out this element of the adventure you are on, of opening your heart again or keeping it open as you get through the hard times in your life.

2. Reread the passage on page 94 and add some details that make it more personal to your life and circumstances. Be positive. Be hopeful. Be encouraging to yourself, even if it doesn't feel natural. Embrace your inner storyteller and remember we don't have to believe every detail in a story to give the story our attention. Use it as a visual meditation and read it aloud with your additions, embracing the potential in the vision and the words. Take gentle, deep breaths as you do this.

3. Write about something fear-inducing you have imagined for yourself that didn't come true. What would you say is your 'disempowering story', if you could summarise it in a few words, and what do you feel about it presently in your life?

CHAPTER SEVEN

The Power of Grief

The Great Mess feels ominous, not just because it's full of challenge and discomfort, but because we haven't paid enough attention to how capable we have proven ourselves to be to even get to this very day (and through all the messes that are now behind us). Often, we are too engaged in the habits outlined in Part One. Because a lot of our thinking and feeling time is caught up in these, we haven't acknowledged the grit, resourcefulness and determination in our spirits that are intuitively activated under such circumstances to support and help transport us through them. We also give none or little time or attention to how capable we might become through this new engagement with the Great Mess. There are more significant details and features in the vision before us than just the setback ahead (like what we are made of and our success rate with certain variables thus far), but, instead, all the time and attention we have quite instinctively gets caught up in spinning thoughts about the threat. We get so locked into the suffering involved in what we have faced or are facing, how scary it appears and sometimes is, and what might be lost through it, that we forget to also take into deeper consideration the very person who has shown endurance, strength and bravery in similar experiences in the past. And because of that fact (which can be backed up with evidence) this person is also a force to contend with. Their only serious fault or flaw is that they don't realise that yet. Because they define themselves by the thousands of things they will feel and see outside of themselves, rather than what they demonstrate day in and day out. They will define themselves by what they don't yet possess or have lost beforehand, rather than focus in on what they do have. Yes, this is you and me – we all do it.

I have always been intrigued by the dexterity and depth of the human spirit that only becomes readily accessible and translucent in times of uncertainty and upheaval. Yet, the capacity to survive, adapt, persist and even thrive under harsh conditions often feels like such a recurring enigma that, when we look back on the most difficult times in our lives, we can't quite put into words what it was that got us through. At the point of entry into the menacing fog of instability, all we could see and feel was the looming impossibility hanging over our heads. To not collapse under the pressure. To not burn, melt or burst in the flames. To not lose ourselves forever in the inescapable obscurity. To not get eaten alive by the dragon or trampled by the ogre. But, somehow, we manage to get by, move through and travel on, until the next inferno stops us in our step. And we often do it with little awareness of the marvel at play: that innate subtle genius inside the human heart that has the uncanny propensity to transform the ugly into some kind of beautiful and the harshest conditions into something deeply meaningful.

We are asleep to the deeper workings of this under-the-skin networking of our intuitive intelligence that is activated under pressure. The immediate pain and distress the potholes and hellholes bring justifiably distract us. But then we reach the latest footpath of any new calamity, hardly any more alert to the mechanism of strength, adaptability and creativity we automatically lean on in times of challenge, and that we have relied on in most of our previous setbacks. Every superhero knows that if you don't understand your power, you cannot skilfully use it. As the hero of your own story, and this particular adventure, this is also true. Understanding is the match to light your fire. Understanding with action is a match made in heaven.

∾

You don't realise that you are a force to contend with,
because something else is always occupying your view.

∾

There are lots of reasons why we get so entangled in this automatic approach, one in particular I want to look at next. But right now, I simply want to distinguish this imbalance in our vision as one of the understated, yet primary reasons why we get so intimidated by life. Our focus is fixated on disempowering details. And with a growing awareness of this and why and how it happens, we can turn this variable around to make it work for us. We can start to focus on empowering details. When this happens, it slowly changes everything.

AN UNLIKELY GAME CHANGER

Learning how to grieve is directly and chiefly entwined in the process of shifting our focus so that we can eventually see ourselves more clearly and positively in an integral way. Situations and events randomly and suddenly occur, where we lose people, relationships, opportunities, experiences and objects that are incomparably valuable to us. Until we learn how to grieve the many unprocessed memories and emotions that feel blocked inside us, these past encounters with loss impact our vision of self and life, arguably more than anything else. Yes, I am suggesting that the way you see the Great Mess is largely impacted by what you haven't yet fully grieved over, and in all dealings with the mess, these unprocessed feelings we carry instead are what are first triggered, and they immediately become our filter to interpret current life by. For example, you are in a relationship with someone and have recently moved out of the 'honeymoon' period, and you are in the midst of your first serious argument. You also had a fractured childhood because your parents got divorced and it felt like the two most important people in your life who made up a loving dream team suddenly became sworn enemies overnight. You haven't grieved the loss involved in your parents separating because as a child you felt you had no choice but to just go along with it, but your memories of abandonment and neglect are immediately triggered through this argument, and you can only see that the destination up ahead is a bitter break-up. You are projecting the unprocessed loss you felt over your parents' divorce on to this sticky moment between you and your partner, so that you can't see it clearly in its own right. If you could see it clearly, maybe the outcomes of this disagreement wouldn't feel so dramatic and unsparing. Maybe they could turn out to be positive and offer an opportunity to get to know each other better and strengthen your intimacy, commitment and intrigue in one another.

It's also important to note that when I mention grief, I am suggesting the process belonging to it, all of its dimensions, of feeling through emotions evoked by the loss and then slowly making peace and finding closure in these tender emotional landscapes. The activity in these landscapes, conscious and subconscious, directly filters into your everyday experience. Over the years, I have understood grief as the passageway through and out of feeling so lost because of loss. And it's important to distinguish the two. I am not advocating that we need to lose and suffer more in our lives, but I am suggesting that we need to learn to grieve over what we lose, as a way to integrate the harsher experiences of life and not be held down by them.

∽

Sadness has taught me things that happiness just can't, like in the same way the daylight can't teach me about the stars.

∽

Let me explain further. Grief is a bridge that allows us to walk alongside prevailing details of our past and all we feel about them in our inner worlds, so that we can gradually comprehend, process and release our grip on them, and in return they no longer dictate or formulate how we see ourselves. As we take grief's hand, we can slowly relieve ourselves of the heaviness of emotions and longings inside by giving them permission to emerge, so that, eventually, when we do look in, we can see ourselves undistorted, from the shadows of all we have suffered already.

Grief is perhaps the most undervalued and misunderstood recurring experience and point of life-changing catharsis in any human story. If we knew better how to process grief beyond the initial scope of shattering feeling and purposeful function it offers us – if we saw it as a way to connect with the expressed and unexpressed love, truth and desire we hold for the people, chapters and things we lose along the way – I am certain our attitude towards the messy chapters in our lives would transform.

USING GRIEF TO OPEN YOUR HEART

It is helpful to distinguish grief as something different to loss, because they are sometimes presented as synonymous to each other, when one (the grief) is actually the response and resolution of the devasting impact of the other (the loss). Grief can actually become a tool to move through loss. If we can feel through, beyond the natural resentment and shock we feel, the grief and emotional stirrings evoked in any bereavement emerge as a guide through the foggy and brutal wasteland of devastation and desolation. We treat grief like it is the loss itself when it is actually more. Grief combines the loss, the release, you and your relationship to whatever you have lost, in addition to who you can become, through and because of it, and even the evolution of your relationship too.

I began my learnings with grief and bereavement as an adult, in the early spring of 2016, when I suffered my first (late) miscarriage and lost my little girl at the beginning of my second trimester. It was the biggest mess of my life to date; the greatest inducer of trauma, old and new. It owned every reason under the sun as to why I should shut down from it and avoid the pain for as long as possible. But in light of the immense devastation I felt, that was simply impossible.

We all have a strong memory of an event or two or three that we remember as the main tragedy to hurl us away from everything we once knew. They are the blind spots along our path, where we can't even sense the catastrophe looming up ahead. When you have felt death happen from inside of you and still you live to tell the tale, because someone else died instead of you, everything collapses. You lose yourself in a warped vortex of survivor's guilt. The aching paradox of baby loss has you throttling old truths you once lived by, because nothing makes sense anymore. It's not only baby loss that does this. That intensity of confusion, loss and rage can follow from a whole collection of harsh experiences, like the death of a loved one, a life-changing illness or accident or the conclusive breakdown of or betrayal in a long-term relationship. It's the kind of experience not only are you totally unprepared for, but you're not even the slightest bit privy to that gravity of emotion beforehand.

It shocks you to your core. Your happy place becomes an entrance into hell. It's like post-bomb devastation within you, full of contradiction, mind-fuckery and paradox. You implode from the inside. And you are left with millions of pieces of your identity, belief system and memory bank splattered on the soil of your life that at first you can't help but stamp on, in disbelief, in fury, in sorrow. But the shock soon enough disarms you. Time is a blur. You are surrounded by fog. The screams are silenced in the shock. You become nobody in that very moment. And, eventually, as the loss becomes you, you realise out of all this piercing pain, you are given a bulb of opportunity to rebuild all these demolished areas inside you any way you want, without any of the falsehoods and conditioning of before, if, indeed, you want to. This was miscarriage for me. But maybe it was something else that made you feel this way.

It was the first time in my life I couldn't just shut down and direct my attention elsewhere. I couldn't 'bury my head in the sand'. I couldn't get over-busy to become distracted. I couldn't do anything that stopped me from feeling it all — each particle of the internal demolition — because it had all happened in my body. The tragedy that severed us from one another was all I had to work with, to find something of my unborn little girl that I could still hold on to. Trying to shut down the feelings felt like shutting down all I had left of her. A child who my body had already given up, without any say-so from me. A child I was never going to hold or smell or look into. And all my body wanted was to feel bound to this little creature again, in the wake of giving her up. So, it didn't let me close off, for too long anyway. In fact, my body was all she and I had left in common. I had been her home for a short while. My body was still my home. I have been through a lot of hard times (as we all have), but this was my first encounter with the darker aspects of life at this kind of intensity when I didn't try to close my heart as a way of preserving myself. And this entire, excruciatingly painful chapter of processing my loss, established on this unfamiliar, harsh and bleak ground of miscarriage, gradually and literally transformed my world. To the point that, since then, I have tried to keep my heart open, no matter what storm has come to my doorstep.

I opened my heart in the midst of the mess, to stay true and conscious of my changing feelings, as much as I could; to process, honour and acknowledge this strange place and time of reckoning and catharsis I had found myself in (and would never wish upon another). I wasn't going to commit to any introspective learning and healing through the gaze of retrospect like I had done with all other storms in my past. And, don't get me wrong, this kind of integrative learning is useful and invigorating in its own right. It's the only way to deal with old trauma and difficulties. But this time was different. It was fresh and I was more integrated. This wasn't just something to put my head down in and only survive. I was going to learn, purge, heal and grow actively on the go. I wanted to engage, to be involved, to walk with all the trauma, the pain, the emptiness. It was all I had left of her and us. I wasn't going to cut off for the unforeseen future. I wasn't going to avoid myself. And that's when the power of mess opened up a new way to me. I took the mess of my life as the ground to consciously make a temporary home upon. And gradually it showed itself to be my most significant rite of passage yet.

A lot of moving through the grief was raw, painful and dark, but I *felt* peculiarly alive in most of the processing and the recovery. Even in the episodes when I felt like I was in between worlds, not really here and totally lost when I thought of existence, over there, behind the veil. Even in the seeming cruelty of the loss and emptiness, I experienced some extreme highs through realisations that left me feeling transcendental. The extreme lows were brutal and unforgiving, but they played their part in my waking up to myself. Waking myself up out of years of feeling estranged from parts of who I was, that I had even forgotten I had lost touch with. Parts of myself that previous awakenings and breakdowns hadn't located or acknowledged. There was life in the pain, in feeling it through, with my heart open and willing, rather than running from it. There was connection. And I kept being honest with it all. I didn't try to 'get the grieving process right'. I didn't try to be 'good' or rush through it.

There were weeks and months when I was bursting with rage and experiencing genuinely ugly feelings that were a challenge to manage in a wholesome and responsible way. But I committed to not turning away, for too long at least. I committed to not avoiding or punishing the parts of me that felt broken and bitter or that I might have blamed years before. And so, there was life and love in the aching, as my heart desperately looked for ways to find her again, somehow. Honouring my feelings solidified my presence here in the world. It gave me a reason to stand up and not hide away. It felt deeply meaningful, to be suspended in my mourning for however long the passage through the grief took. It also clarified deep truths and what was important in my life. It gave me the resolve to finally (and easily) let go of the insignificant details of living that had taken up too much time and space in my mind. These were things I hadn't even realised were holding me back until now.

I am indeed a student of grief. Perhaps you are too. Loss isn't only death, and we all carry some kind of burden of loss that hangs over our personal expression and vision of the world until we learn to move through it, and in fact beyond it, into further landscapes of living. If we don't become students of grief, we remain under the heavy hand of our losses, wounded and somewhat trapped, resigned to be haunted by the pain of the loss instead. But there are profound lessons in the loss that promise a transformation in thought and vision. And we can't access them until we start getting honest with our messy feelings. Our honesty is tied into those realisations, like a bridge connecting two cliff sides. This, in a nutshell, is the process and helping hand of grief. It is a means of essentially emptying out our hearts. It is a way for us to build that bridge of honesty towards the eventual realisations by working through the pain, the confusion, the resentment and the fear, evoked through the losses. We can then fill our hearts with enriched, integrative and expansive truths that were impossible to sense or see before, for being so full up with the aftermath of the loss itself. In fact, opening our hearts again implies getting honest with ourselves and working through our messy feelings about the difficult happenings in our passage through life.

∾

Processing our grief is a critical component
on the path to peace and empowerment.

∾

It's how rebirths happen. For example, you have gone through a horrible break-up of a long-term relationship and you feel your life is falling through your hands like sand, as you lose a sense of identity and certainty that has kept everything in place for the longest while.

But then you surrender to the seeming earthquake and you get right up close to everything that has shattered, and you process how it feels to have lost your grip on life. Over time you realise that maybe you don't have to hold on to life with the tight grip that you once did, and you start to let go of the reasons you personally held on so tightly in the first place. As a result, you learn to let go of elements in life that you can't control or that have weighed down heavy on you for some time. There is a new experience of life settling into your bones. This is the rebirth – a new way to experience yourself is opening up in your cells. You start to feel alive in ways you haven't done before, because you are no longer clenching your fists. You have less tension in your body and your mind. You realise you never wanted to hold on so tightly in the first place. You just learnt to do that in order to survive some harsh moments in your past. And now you don't have to continue doing so. It's also clearer to see the things you want to do. Grief opens up portals of freedom I am not sure we can find any other way. It's why love and loss go together.

I also believe that if and when you open your heart to grief, when in the grip of loss, no amount of mess can ever close it again because the combination of grief with an open heart makes for a transformative combo, of proportions we have nothing to compare it to. The Great Mess is what causes a lot of the losses we will encounter along the way, but grief opens a way through it, and into perhaps the most integrated, wholesome and responsive way of living there is. But, yes, it is hard at the beginning, and everything hurts. And learning to embrace and sit with the uncomfortable feelings inside us is both courageous and admirable. If we don't, they will continue to control what we see when we look out into the world and also when we look inside. They will stop us from seeing what we need to see.

My stepdad passed away during the writing of this book. He died on the eve of Thanksgiving. That Thanksgiving would also have marked the twenty-fifth wedding anniversary of my mum and him. It has felt incredibly sad ever since. And I am yet to be pulled into the depths of grief over not having him in this world anymore, because, quite frankly, I am still in shock. But the sadness, the disbelief, the emptiness, they are all there underneath the soil of my everyday happenings. At the time of his funeral, I changed my Facebook profile picture to one of him. Now, every time I log on, I see his blue eyes and it twinges. I am reminded. He's gone. My mum is widowed. I miss knowing that he's around. Everything has changed. It twinged so hard one day that I went to take the photo down. But that's not sitting with the uncomfortable feelings. That's not letting the grief do its work. That was me about to shut down a little. So, I held back and he is still there, seemingly as me on Facebook, and I am letting the pain be what it is as I tread gently into this landscape of loss again. Because loss is on the other side of love. You can't have love without loss somewhere down the line. Eventually love is the very thing to hold the loss in place. And, right now, the pain is only confirmation of that love too.

I know it's not easy to let that kind of depth of pain up to the surface and not stuff it back inside a secret chamber of your heart. It's important not to rush through your feelings or try to pretend you are OK when you are not. The initial intensity of the pain in grief has a lifespan. It won't last forever, but you have to allow it to be in your conscious thought and feeling until the intensity starts to simmer down. It's often at this point that it goes into a process of transmutation, to teach you something invaluable, rather than just feel bleak and hurtful. But not shutting off to it through the period where it does just feel bleak and severe is tough. Talking out your feelings in this time can be very helpful, even as you imagine you won't find the right words to express this kind of brokenness. Not isolating yourself and being reachable and contactable by those who have your back is also really important, even though you will often feel like you just want to cut yourself off from the surrounding world. Grief has many faces. It's just important to not put a lid on how it comes up for you. It comes up to take you on a journey, into your deepest honesty, breaking through all the walls in your mind and around your heart. And not obstructing it as it shows up is how you walk with it.

THE MAGIC OF GRIEF

You have probably never put those words together. Grief is many things, but to refer to it like it's got some magic inside of it is an odd thing to suggest and, as I do, I am in no way making light of any grief that you, dear reader, might be carrying. But the essence and power of grief is something we are taught very little about while growing up. We are also not taught that, just as the means to create diamonds from carbon deposits requires exceedingly high temperatures, so can the best in us and of life be eventually produced under a similar kind of pressure; the kind of pressure we feel in holding heavy emotions and dealing with life when it seems to take from us what we have, want or find deeply meaningful.

Leaning on this clichéd parallel a little while longer, I am suggesting the carbon deposits to be representative of the darker experiences we go through. But what I am also suggesting is that the heat required to transmute those experiences resides in the process of grief itself, of prising or keeping our heart open to go through all that's in there. But often, because of the pain we are in, and in fear of feeling even more, we keep the act of processing the pain at bay. So, we tend to only experience the surface level of grief. And then we stop. We feel the pain, but we don't metabolise it. And yet the magic of grief can only happen in the metabolism. Until you begin processing the pain you are in, you just remain on the hard brunt of it. And you build up a backlog of unprocessed heavy feeling that will at some point burst through in ways you can't readily control. It also remains the unconscious filter for how we comprehend the world around us, right down to our everyday circumstances.

Actively digesting difficult experiences guided by the grief we feel over them is the process needed to make sense of harsh and unforgiving moments. Again, talking out your thoughts and feelings (even if you just think they're gibberish) can transport you into this. Asking yourself questions, reflecting, journaling and writing letters, participating in activities that are connected to who or what you are grieving over (like visiting familiar places, listening to certain music or contemplating certain memories) also help create the bridge you need to walk on. We grieve more and carry more grief than we realise, because we have all lost. And I have wondered if this is the reason why, when you get to grips with this aspect of life, it can yield the most healing and transformative realisations and free you in ways you might not have even known you needed to be freed. Just because it is so universal. It takes up such a huge portion of all the experiences we will go through. Find the most loving, illuminated, responsive and integrated people you know, and I bet you they have both lost a lot and learnt to grieve those losses through their lives.

Grief has an incomparable power to draw you closer to yourself, even just on the simple level that, in the face of loss, we tend to turn inwards. In that, you are given a bridge to better understand yourself and really learn how to own your life and how you honestly want to express it in this world. Because you are slapped with the reality of impermanence, you learn how to own your love and get honest with how you want to convey it in the world also. *This* is perhaps the most meaningful and powerful choice you will ever make in your life: *how to own and convey your love*. And to make it from the most honest, vulnerable and lucid aspects of your self is something we all desire. I would actually define the meaning of life as a rite of passage to that exact goal. And there is no better fulfilment than when you reach that valiant objective. Honouring your grief can get you closer to that destination than you might imagine. And it can water all the flowers you pass by on the way.

This really stands as a revolutionary proposition. Could it be that the way to move forward in your life is to turn up the heat in your heart and mind by getting honest with any unprocessed grief you carry? Yes, I am suggesting exactly this – this is also the act of opening your heart once again. Stop running away from the sadness you carry. Stop numbing yourself to it. Stop distracting yourself and pretending it's not there. I also need to state here that this doesn't mean you are signing your life away to annual cycles of sorrow, despondency and feeling like life is basically a meaningless tyranny. This is the surface of grief (and the most unpleasant part of it). But beneath it is an unpredictable and extraordinary process of transformation where you learn how to integrate the deepest and most powerful aspects of who you are and all you have been through into your conscious life, and leave behind what you are not. Grief prompts you to stop getting so caught up in the things of life that just waste your precious time. Grief washes through you so that you eventually learn to meet life in your authenticity rather than in the facades and webs you were caught in before.

RECONCEPTUALISING GRIEF

In walking with grief for many years, I have started to reconceptual-ise it and imagine grief to be a dark goddess hovering over the voids in people's hearts, much like Hades sails through the underworld. It has helped me surrender more quickly when I feel the force of abstract emotions rush through me at random points in the day. I imagine at these points that it is grief knocking on the door of my heart and it paints any interaction in a hue of deeper purpose and intimacy.

Being on the end of her heavy hand many a time and feeling entirely alone in her presence for months on end, I decided that trying to grow a relationship with her was the most useful connection I could forge. I got to know the mechanisms of grief in a deep and introspective way. I was able to craft out a kind of life-giving energy in all the processing of life-losing that encapsulates such heart-shattering emotions. And I became deeply respectful of the companionship and this new thoughtfulness I felt forming with the grief in my heart and all it was teaching me. As we've seen, your imagination is a wonderful tool to use. Don't be scared to play with these ideas as well.

All the untrue stories you have believed about yourself and your life through the years can be left by the wayside. Walk with your grief and you will find it doesn't break you. It breaks the walls around your heart that you've always thought were you, but really, they have just been fencing you in. Walk with grief and it will strip every-thing back and soften the ground that the seeds of your dreams have been laid in. It reaches right into your centre to make your heart and soul wholly accessible, so that the light can get in and out freely, without so many obstacles.[1] Like Mizuta Masahide once exclaimed in a Haiku:

Since my house burned down
I now own a better view
Of the rising moon[2]

It can often feel like a cruel formula – that struggle might lead to deeper freedom; that collapse might lead to a rebirth of your wildest dreams; and that the prelude of any great healing is unfathomable pain. But to imagine that there might be something beautiful on the end of your suffering can at least offer a little motivation to keep trying to get through the tough moments, and to keep trying to open your heart in honesty and eventually hope. In the same way the day leads into the night and the night leads into the day, there is an uncanny and irrefutable relationship between dark and difficult moments and the brightened shifts in perspective and heart space they can bring. This is not to say that the dark times are a guarantee to brighter days, but the possibility is always there, not as pressure to push you into an excavation for truth, but as inspiration, to offer a little hope, especially on the darkest days when you are engulfed. Even more than that, the pain can at some point make the suffering feel like a worthwhile experience, and we won't then be so intimidated by it, if and when it emerges.

I've come to comprehend that this deficit in understanding the nature and purpose of grief is one of the biggest influences on the way in which we approach difficult moments in life. And if we were to develop a new attitude towards this process of deep emotion we try to keep at bay for as long as we can, we would interpret the messy chapters in our lives so very differently, because a lot of what we have to face evolves around loss to some degree. And encountering loss can eventually evolve to be transformational.

Given that grieving is such a huge part of our experiences as human beings, it is often the elephant in the room that we pretend to look through. And yet, if we were shown how to ride upon it, it would take us to richer and more meaningful life experiences. When someone asks us if we are OK, we need to dare to be honest and say we are not. We need to keep talking about those we have loved and lost. We need to stop putting on smiles when our hearts are breaking. We have to learn to feel through our feelings, which means we have to stop doing the things that hold us back from feeling those emotions – all the control, the suppression, the self-gaslighting, the avoidance, the overindulgence and the numbing.

∽

There's no tiptoeing around grief. The
way out is always through.

∽

Grief wants to get you to your most honest self, beyond all the masks, beyond all the habits, beyond all the judgements, so that you can experience yourself and your life in a transcendental way.

As you integrate the occasional voyages with grief into your life, it is true that you are also then surrendering to feeling twinges of pain, small or notable regrets here and there. But they act like a limp of the heart you are willing to live with. Because they are proof you have made it through the darkest, most ominous passages of assimilating the harsher experiences in life. They are proof you can do the hard stuff and therefore your confidence in yourself will inevitably grow. The landscape of grief eventually leads to planes of existing that embolden everything profound remaining in your life, boosting them to glisten in a new light. And we have to commit and stay on its path of catharsis until it does. It fortifies your relationships and valued connections (all that makes you feel wholesomely connected and gives you a sense of belonging in this world), much like the Japanese art of kintsukuroi that restores broken pottery with powdered gold, and so honouring its history, rather than hiding it.

Write it out

1. What have you learnt through grief and loss so far? Have you experienced a softer side of grief as you have tried to come to terms with things you have gone through or does it just feel like hostile terrain you don't want to explore?

2. I believe that, on a daily basis, whether we like it or not, we are dealing with matters of loss as much as we deal with matters of love; whether it be about actual loss or what we don't want to lose (or fail at), about how to prevent loss or how to move on from it. Where do you think you stand with loss at the moment? Is it a big part of your life and your thinking patterns? Does it scare you? Do you feel surrendered to it? Write down a few things that you feel you have lost over your lifetime. How does it make you feel?

3. Write a list of the hard moments you are going through and see if you can link them to the angle of grief and loss explored in this chapter.

CHAPTER EIGHT

The Gift of Reassurance: Everything is Going to be OK

When I find myself in the grip of my own panic, anxiety or a difficulty that has demanded something from me that I was yet to discover about myself, one simple phrase has meant more than any other wisdom under the sun: '*It is going to be OK.*'

This statement is simple, arguably oversimplified and overused. It can be annoying to hear on some occasions too. Yet, in essence, it is still powerful. And there is no harm in trying to incorporate something that is simple, harmless, potentially powerful and definitely straightforward into our fundamental thinking and feeling.

When in the grip of fear, nothing is more helpful than positive presence and reassurance. And this statement, seeming so straightforward and simple on the outset, is actually a gateway to a whole new world of experience. It's like the wardrobe in C. S. Lewis' beloved *The Lion, The Witch and The Wardrobe*. Walk through it (explore it) or even hide in it awhile (sit with the meaning, digesting it) and you are bound for a world of illuminating possibilities, magical happenings, ever-evolving marvels and extraordinary undertakings. The statement 'It is going to be OK' is the entry point into learning how to parent your heart, which is fundamental to any healing passage or journey of emotional development.

We can live in a spiral of stifling hypervigilance, the kind of tension that permeates and weakens everything, keeping you on edge all the time. You feel sick to your stomach. It wears you down, so that you become stifled and muted in your self-expression. It's the worst of fear, always leaving you feeling exposed and defenceless. And it can turn into an existence, albeit a draining and horrendous one, that you can become all too familiar with. You live in a constant state of looking over your shoulder for fear of being attacked or otherwise everything falling apart.

Once fear has invaded and drained the life out of you, then severe demoralisation seizes your soul and your perception. This is a harsh reality to survive. It leaves you unable, hopeless and, eventually and naturally so, you start to estimate most of life to be entirely threatening and hostile, even when it isn't. And if this *is* your reality and you have completed the task of surviving it up to now, you are amazing and far stronger than you realise.

'Everything is going to be OK' is the first thing I always tell my daughters when I find them emotional or overwhelmed by something. I hug them and that hug is an expression of the same reassurance. My eldest daughter actually confessed a couple of years ago that, when she was younger, she would hit our coffee table with her hand and start fake crying, until my husband would run in to see what was wrong. She would then lie and say she banged her head, just so that he would pick her up in his arms and stroke her hair, telling her gently that everything was going to be OK, over and over again. We have giggled about it numerous times since, and I think the kind of hugs that accompany the words 'Everything is going to be OK', when genuinely communicated, are often more potent than a simple hug without them.

In a similar vein to what my eldest girl confessed, we all too have a little person inside us who occasionally comes to the surface, looking for that kind of reassurance. I believe that need is lifelong. We don't grow out of it. We can just learn to better integrate it into our intimate relationships and our relationship with self, without feeling the need to simulate some kind of dramatic happening to receive that kind of attention. We don't always have to bang our hands on the coffee table! But that kind of positive feedback offers incredible emotional nourishment. It acts like fuel to our courage. You are never so brave as when you feel loved. And bravery is just what you need when faced head-on with any mess you have to deal with.

There are people in this world who are the walking embodiment of the spirit of 'Everything is going to be OK'. They have this beautiful calm about them and, just by being in their presence, you find yourself exhaling, dropping your shoulders and relaxing a little more. I have always thought that the best kind of love you can offer anyone is when you allow them to be themselves with you. When you make someone feel like everything is going to be OK so that they take their masks off, lower their walls and remove any defences – I don't think there's a better gift to give in all the world. We all need at least one person like that in our lives. And we also need a prolonged period of stability in our years of growing up to reinforce the truth of that statement. But some of us aren't that fortunate. So, we look for that kind of reassurance or anything that marginally resembles it wherever we can. This was the story of my life up until I reached my thirties.

∽

There's no greater expression of love than to be made
to feel you don't have to hide any part of you away.

∽

If this kind of attitude was a vitamin, honestly, I think I have always been deficient. There has always been this background noise behind my smiles – fake and real – over the years. It has been behind my attitude problems. All my drama. My loss of identity. My many stories of finding strange, ill-fitting identities along the way before finally settling in what now has proven to be authentic and enlivening. All the collapses and the shattering. Perhaps even more ironically, it has remained behind the best parts and times of my life, too. And the background noise can be summarised by this kind of friction: '*But what if it's not going to be OK?*' or '*What if/What about when I mess this up?*'

I think nearly all of us share this background anxiety that has a way of often submerging the forefront of our lives as well, because of experiences we had in our childhood that rocked the foundations of this truth to some debilitating degree.

THE REASSURANCE IN RE-PARENTING

To personally comprehend the unique power of these words on your own complex being, you will need to look back on your life story and trace either the absence or presence of them along the pages. You need to remember when you heard those words from someone you loved and relied upon, and imagine how your senses would be enraptured if the spirit behind those words, the profound truth behind them, was the basis of *every* day of your life; how you might perceive the world and what you would listen out for, and all you might then feel.

You need to remember what it felt like to not hear those words when you needed them and the feelings that emerged in their absence. You need to be able to imagine how certain days might have progressed in an opposite direction had you been reassured with the words 'Everything is going to be OK.' Imagine how tall you might have felt, how giant you might have seemed in yourself. How you might have slowed down to smell the flowers, rather than frantically living at a pace that was solely focused on the destination rather than the adventure. How you might have said yes to the challenges ahead, rather than hiding in a corner, announcing your failure before any possible invested action.

This is where the mysterious transformation has grounds to happen. Once you have reflected on how much or how little you have felt those words in your life, you have to be daring enough to take it upon yourself to now become that person to your heart. I know this is quite a leap. I am suggesting that you take on the role that has either been fulfilled or unfulfilled in your life from here on in, but this is what I have learnt in coming to this same point in my own life.

If you keep looking for someone else to fulfil that role of reassurer in your life, your relationships will always be imbalanced and largely disempowering. This essential need is never filled in the way that you alone can fill it once you reach adulthood. That doesn't mean you can't lean on people you love to remind you of this beautiful truth when you have forgotten it or feel too overwhelmed to encourage yourself, but it is no match for replacing a relationship grown with your own heart based on being your own primary source of encouragement. Nobody, not even the closest person to you, can ever know your suffering like you do. And you are with yourself more than anyone else will ever be.

To really adopt the outlook and explore the powers of reassurance (even if you have a hard time considering it could be true), you have to approach it like an experiment or a project. For all the times you find yourself flirting with the possibilities that might occur if every-thing went wrong, you need to give that same time and energy to the idea that everything is going to be OK. Just like with any skill, it will take time to see the benefits. But approach it rationally and work out which slant offers most back to you. You will be surprised how much your heart will eat up those words, the possibilities and energy behind them and the underlying implications. You need to fill up on your tank of reassurance if you are going to venture out into the lands that the Great Mess occupies and return with some incredible stories to tell. In learning to be your own cheerleader and support, you are offering yourself the best of love that nobody can take away from you.

It is imperative that we grow the spirit behind the words 'It's going to be OK' right in the soil of our being if we are going to bloom into the life we are worthy and deserving of. And if you look at those five words and don't know what to do with them, start by repeating them to yourself over and over again, gently, quietly, under your breath, whenever you need to, even if at first you don't believe them; even if it feels wrong and painful to say those words because that hasn't been your experience up to now.

Learning to parent your heart is the most healing thing you will ever do for your life. Learning to be your own support and encouragement – to be the one to rustle up those words whenever you need them – will birth new worlds inside you. It is where all the magic happens. It's the worthy opposition to that inner critic that has had too many days reigning over all the thoughts that transpire inside us. And actually, it has the most potential to usurp that critical voice from its throne, more than any other positive mindset you might integrate as part of your self-care routine along the way. When dealing with the messiness of life, you need to make choices that will dethrone your inner critic and put the maternal voice of reassurance in its place, bit by bit. Begin with replacing 'Everything is going to go wrong' – which is what we often feel when intimidated by coming chaos – with

'Everything is going to be OK'. Consider it enough over time, experiment with it and you will begin to believe it. The spirit behind those words will keep you on the path of love.

Write it out

1. Go back to a time in your life when you needed to hear the words 'Everything is going to be OK.' And then, as you are imagining yourself in that vulnerable position, write a letter to that version of yourself, reassuring yourself with the comforting and calming spirit behind those words.

2. Write another letter to the person you wanted to hear those words from at the time that you have remembered; be really honest about why you wanted to hear them and how it impacted you not to feel them. You are activating the power of honesty in completing these prompts. Unless you decide otherwise, these letters are just for you, although you may want to read them aloud to someone you trust, because there is a magical power in bringing the written and spoken word together.

3. Remember your backpack. Consider something heavy in your bag that you could remove so that you can take this reflection with you on your adventure and give it ample space to support you. It could be the opposite of reassurance, like discouragement and doubt. Choose to focus more on reassuring your heart than discouraging yourself in this new direction. You will feel lighter for not carrying so much.

CHAPTER NINE

The Exhale and the Pause

D o you know that feeling of living like you are constantly holding your breath because you're too scared or too tense or too busy to exhale, and the relaxation and ease we associate with being able to breathe freely feels impossible to access? Of course, you are actually breathing, but it doesn't feel like it. I have written about this state of being, or in fact this state of *non-being*, a lot over the years. You forget to let yourself be. You forget to give yourself a moment to step back, a moment to look up, a moment to feel hopeful. I believe it is a common state of mind in this day and age – always on the go, always looking over your shoulder, always expecting the worst, always feeling like you have too much to do, always keeping your walls up, always feeling overwhelmed because of the countless uncertainties hanging over your head.

I know that way of being well. I wish I didn't. I wish mine was another story to tell. But I have spent too many of my days reminding myself to breathe. I have spent too many days forgetting that I *can* breathe; that I have the right to breathe, away from the struggle and the stress. Yes, that I can always take a moment to catch my breath. It's an unpleasant feeling, when you feel so untrusting of 'the moment' that you won't even let yourself consciously connect with the most natural thing your body does.

The state of mind illustrated in the metaphor of forgetting to breathe and living like you are always holding your breath is basically when you are so caught up in the perceived danger and impossible demands around you that your lungs feel full of liquefied tension. You dissociate from the things that come naturally to you, the very ways of being that enrich your heart and keep you alive (and indeed feeling alive) on the planet. The result is that you feel almost ghost-like, unseen and unconsidered, with nowhere to really belong. Yet, you deal with a tidal wave of apprehension hitting against your ribs and your stomach as you try to live through the days. And every time you might try to take a breath, it feels shallow and weak, like you can't get the whole breath out. It's like somebody has your nervous system by the scruff of the neck. I have to be honest; I hate that feeling of seeming like you might never take a deep breath again.

THE MINDSET OF THE EXHALE

That's why I began forcing myself to take long, deep breaths a few years ago when in the grip of this state of mind, however shallow, forced and weak they felt in the beginning. I used to remind myself that it was something I was allowed to do. I don't know why we think we will survive a harsh encounter or a high-pressured situation better if we hold our breath. Stress does funny things to our minds and then subsequently our bodies. But preventing that breath-held feeling from settling into my bones, by telling myself to do the opposite, and then doing it again and again and again, significantly helped to reduce its effects over time. It helped for obvious reasons, but also because there is a fantastic and empowering mindset behind giving yourself permission to breathe out, to indeed *exhale*.

When I tell myself that the only way to survive this moment is to live as though I am holding my breath, I am also telling myself other things. The list is long, but a few assertions come to mind, like:

- I am powerless.
- I am on my own.
- This moment is unmanageable.
- My safety is threatened.
- I need to escape.

I am aligning myself with the idea that I am unwelcome in this moment and that everything could go wrong and is most likely to. I can summarise all the above by this one statement: *I am simply not enough*.

And please understand that if you find yourself forgetting to breathe right now in your own life, it is a perfectly normal and common reaction to stressful situations and the Great Mess. We all do it. We will all continue to do it. And it's not a state we should ever feel ashamed about. But it's not a healthy long-term emotional pattern to leave as it is. It eats you up and wears you down at the same time. Both you and I deserve better than that. And I firmly believe we can have it. So, finding ways to manage what often feels like an automatic response we have no control over is both insightful and restorative, although it might feel like hard and complicated work at first.

Now, when I give myself permission to breathe, to in fact exhale and stop holding everything in, what I am communicating to my being is something very different. And it's such a beautiful, nourish-ing message that it's worth any time it takes to integrate it into your life (simply by the continual practice of intentionally breathing). As I allow myself to breathe, I am essentially exploring some or all of these mysterious truths:

- I am meant to be here, alive and present in this very moment.
- I am able and I am worthy.
- I will find my way through.
- I am aligning with any possible positive outcomes this moment might produce.
- I can handle this.
- I am supported.
- There is more to my life than the struggle I am dealing with right now.
- There is more for me than any pain or turmoil I am presently in.

Yes, all of this can be found just in your simple breath. Exhaling is a way of giving yourself permission to relax and enter into a communion with life based on trust and growing faith in yourself. It is an invitation to explore further into the story playing out and dig deeper, beyond the initial apparitions conjured up in your mind. It offers an opportunity to loosen your clenched fists and remind yourself you don't have to hold everything inside of you. It makes space for new possibilities and all the positives. It says that maybe, in this moment, you don't have to fear for your life, or for your sanity.

∾

Exhaling operates as a gentle cleanse.

∾

GIVE YOURSELF PERMISSION TO BREATHE

The mindset of the exhale is one of *radical permission* to be in this present moment, rather than wherever else your mind might want to drag you. And I write 'radical' here on purpose, because learning to give ourselves permission to be who we are, to be in this moment, present, open and willing, to believe we are worthy, despite the surroundings, details and possible outcomes, can have a profound and revolutionary impact on how we live every day. We all have our reasons and our stories for why we are the way we are, for why we have our own unique internal battles to face every day. But what keeps us glued to them, more than anything else, is not the reasons why the stories happened and the damage they caused, but because we haven't activated this captivating force of permission yet. We haven't given ourselves permission to step outside these stories through our dreams, our exploration and our efforts. We identify so heavily with these stories and reasons (because this is all we have known for so long) that we cannot imagine there to be different adventures, approaches and beliefs out there for us, or should I say inside us, waiting, dormant, in the spaces of our heart we are yet to discover. We tell ourselves on various levels that the better kind of experiences, adventures and storylines are for someone else, never for us.

Giving ourselves permission to breathe is a wonderful entrance into the arena of empowerment. It is the antithesis of unworthiness. When you give yourself permission to be in this moment, that's how you start to feel present in this moment. When you give yourself permission to be here, you are stepping out of the shadows and asserting that the sun shines for you too. You are worthy of feeling that sun on your face. Giving yourself permission to not be destroyed by the Great Mess, or whatever it is you fear will happen when you face it, is opening up new portals to make passage through. And in them you will be able to transform some of your fundamental thinking. It is the consent you need the most, in order to find new ways of dealing with the complexities at hand, so that they don't suffocate or ruin you, but instead become the guides you need to teach you how to reach into your quiescent strength.

You have to give yourself permission to take the deepest breath whenever you need; whenever you notice your shoulders are tense and your chest is tight. You have to tell yourself you can, and then you have to do it, no matter how alien it feels.

Good times, fulfilling times, meaningful times, finding the rainbow-after-the-storm times, seasons of worthiness and healing and joy and courage and life-shifting focus . . . all the good stuff begins with permission. And permission begins with exhaling.

TAKE THE PRESSURE OFF WHERE YOU CAN

In these times, you always have further to go and too many things to do, and the feeling of overwhelm is constantly hovering over your head. We are bombarded with subtle and blatant messages about where we are meant to be in life. Now, more than ever, the concept of pausing, slowing down and unrushing is vital to the well-being of our minds, bodies and spirits. I have the same affinity for my made-up word 'unrush' as I do with 'exhale'.

Sometimes it's in exhaling that we realise we can slow everything down and, sometimes, in slowing down, we are better able to exhale. Pausing time is a superpower I've always been envious of. I remember watching an American sitcom when I was growing up called *Out of This World*. It was about a teenager who was half alien, and she could pause time. There was something captivating each time she did this. The quiet it created. The space to think and to process what was going on. The way she could get right up close to important details from different angles. The opportunity it created to direct positive outcomes in dramatic situations. It was so appealing to me and has remained so ever since, as I have continuously tried to make home in what I call the 'season of the pause'.

It's when you get to a point in your life when you realise you can't live your life like anyone else so why chase the dreams that were never yours to chase in the first place? Why try to live by someone else's story about you? It's when you work out a pace of life you can manage and still nurture your faculties, rather than existing on a hamster wheel that constantly drains you of your mental and emotional resources. This is the kind of experience of life I imagine where our heart's song can be readily heard because we are not lost in the noisy streets of beeping cars and bustling people, all trying to reach somewhere they are not even sure they want to be anymore. In the pause, I am removed from the grip of my worry, my drive and any tension that might be dominating the present moment.

In the pause, you surrender rather than cling to things with rigid fingers. Your nervous calculating is dissolved because the wind underneath you is enough. The rabbit holes you often get lost down become small dots on a canvas of hope and a colourful, ever-extending horizon. In the pause, you feel what it's like to really be alive. You are alive more than just feeling like you are surviving. You are authentically living more than you are hiding. The framework of the pause is where we all belong, because we realise we are part of something miraculous, and that miracle lives in our very eyes and through the pulsing of our hearts, not in how well we get through our 'things-to-do' list every day.

How do you enter into the season of the pause? If I am right in thinking you are asking this question, you might be surprised by the answer. I was relieved when it dawned on me. Again, it all begins with *permission*.

∽

You have to start giving yourself
permission to pause, to unrush.

∽

Feeling like you can saunter every now and again, and mindfully observe life around you, is a mental health necessity that takes time for us to own. But here is the perspective and feeling to explore: there is nowhere you have to get to in a rush. And actually living life in a rush is unequivocally catastrophic for us in the long run. It's wholesomely better to approach any journey feeling fully present, rather than being preoccupied with the destination all the time – or feeling that we are constantly missing out on something because we are not quick enough to attain it.

Often when facing a messy situation, because of all that it triggers emotionally, we feel a sense of urgency to just get through it, to get it over and done with, to move on as fast as we can. We are faced with huge questions, and we feel the pressure to find the answers immediately. We want to solve the conundrum, not just because that's what we are supposed to do, but because we don't like to be in that state of 'in between' where there is a strong sense of uncertainty hovering over all possible outcomes.

So, the concept of pausing in our busy and troubled circumstances also extends to alleviate the sense of pressure to mend everything right away, to get everything cleaned up and all problems resolved. It counters the assumption of perceived threat that has us feeling as though we need to escape and remedy issues quickly. And it carves out space to breathe, to indeed practise the mindset of the exhale. When facing any messy situation, remembering that answers and resolutions don't have to be found straight away creates a sense of spaciousness, so that we can better benefit from any hidden possibilities and illuminating details available to us in making passage through the circumstance. It also prevents the distorted messages we might assume as truth when in the grip of trying to end a hard moment prematurely. When in a rush, there is a lot of information we don't process. Slowing down offers you the best likelihood of picking up on all the significant details that are most beneficial to you, but could be easily missed.

Offering yourself regular breaks from surrounding tension, complexity and challenges, through exhaling and taking pressure off yourself to resolve circumstances in a short period of time, are also self-kindness practices and a way in which to establish the spirit of self-kindness in the soil of your life. Self-kindness has many faces and offers many avenues in how it can be expressed, but it is a means of compassion directed inwards, best shown in times of trouble and distress. It is essential for a wholesome experience of life, and it is crucial to get into the habit of showing kindness to yourself when you are facing something difficult. The best way to do this is to just get into the habit full stop.

Begin your passage through any arduous obstacle with the mindset of exhaling and the art of unrushing in your pocket, and whatever mountain it is that you have to climb or whatever thorny grounds you have to get over will feel far more doable.

Write it out

1. I have always loved the word 'exhale'. It's one of those words that has a bewitching effect the more you say it. You find yourself embodying its meaning without even realising it, as though locked in a spiritual spell. Try it for me right now. Say 'ex-h-ale' out loud, slowly, taking your time and making sure you say the entire word over and over again, and note if it pulls you in a gently hypnotising way to at least slow down or become more conscious of your breathing in this moment. It might even have you taking deeper breaths. I find the fusion of sounds in the word has a gentle, mesmeric effect. What do you think? Are there any other words that put a kind of spell on you? Write them down.

2. When was the last time you felt like you were living in a state of the exhale? Write about a time where you felt relaxed and like you were not looking over your shoulder all the time. Maybe you haven't felt that for a long time. Imagine what it would be like if you felt like you could breathe freely in your life. How do you think you would approach relationships, conversations and time spent alone?

3. What do the words 'radical permission' conjure up in your mind? Write down your first thoughts about it. What do you feel you can give yourself permission to experience or imagine in your life right now?

CHAPTER TEN

Positive Self-Talk: Why 'Maybe' is a Magical Word

I n times of high stress, we look for ways to dilute the intensity or direct it outside of us because it feels too heavy to carry. Shouting is one of those outlets or taking the opportunity to follow through with a burst of anger. Sometimes internally shouting ourselves down feels like a way to alleviate or at least do something with and control in some way the stress that we are trying to handle or manage. It temporarily feels more emboldening, although it is a pseudo kind of empowerment. It is a fracturing defence mechanism where we turn the conflict we feel on ourselves. Expressing anger makes you feel less vulnerable. We will often choose channels of communication that make us feel less fragile because we want to minimise the discomfort in feeling. But pulling away from the urge to shout ourselves down all the time, as a toxic but temporary way of dealing with pressure, is a necessary practice if we are going to empower ourselves and build a healthy relationship with self that we can make the foundation of our lives. If we have a healthy relationship with self, we can craft out healthy relationships with everything, including the Great Mess.

Over the years, my readers have often commented on the gentle tone that comes through my writing and asked me why I spend so much time suggesting we go gentler on ourselves, especially in the way we talk to ourselves. It's because, generally speaking, it's the one thing we find almost impossible to do. It's because I screamed myself down for years and years – to the point that I was shell-shocked, shaking, always waiting for some kind of bomb to go off inside me. One day I realised I was dying inside. Dying. You don't shout at anyone who's dying. You talk to them gently. So, I started talking to myself in a kinder way. And soon enough it felt like a tone, evoked an internal ambience and created a certain kind of language that could get me back into living once again. And it did exactly that. There is no more powerful voice in this world than the one you use to talk to yourself with. There are no more powerful words in this world than the ones you use in discourse with your own heart, mind and body. This encapsulates a far more powerful dynamic than any roar, growl or sting from any difficult moment that comes your way.

THE MAGIC IN 'MAYBE'

Words are tools. They are building blocks. They are gateways. They are treasure chests, containing possibilities for irreplaceable connection, expression and epiphanies. I have truly experienced my mind suddenly be transported into another world before me that I had no idea existed before, simply because of the energy, the careful depiction and skilful arrangement of certain, powerful words. Words make us laugh and cry. They keep us awake at night and sometimes send us to sleep. They can induce both trauma and healing. They can usher in new beginnings and slam doors shut forever. Words are mysteriously wired to our imaginations and activate them in uncanny ways.

They set free the monsters in our minds, and they can induce the sleeping hero in us all.

༄

You need the right collection of words and the worlds they will open you to in your backpack, when you venture out into the Great Mess of life.

༄

Don't get paranoid about the words you tend to lean on when expressing your feelings or trying to find your way, but do become *mindful* of the words you use. Become curious and reflective over the dialogues you have with yourself and the way you tend to talk about yourself. I always emphasise how important articulation is in any passage of healing and/or self-development. The words we have explored already offer a meaningful new beginning in how to manage your days and moments leading up to facing something you would rather not. You need that simple statement of six words and all it implies – 'Everything is going to be OK'. You need the words *exhale* and *unrush* and the approaches to life they encapsulate. And you also need another word . . . *maybe*.

Maybe is the one word that will pull your heart open after being shut tight for years. It is the word that can remove the full stops from your life. It is the word that can usher in a new dawn after months of being lost in the shadows. It can be the launcher, propelling you boldly towards your dragon and with great faith in yourself, rather than always being on the run and going into hiding because of it. 'Maybe' is another super word and it is at its most miraculous when used like this:

It feels like this horrible period of my life will never end, but maybe *that's not actually true.* Maybe *everything will turn around.*

It feels like I will never be able to get free from this tension, but maybe *there is a way out or a way through, and I just can't see it yet.* Maybe *it's closer than I think.*

I don't think I will get over this, but maybe *I might feel differently about this someday.*

I deserve all the bad things that happen to me, but maybe *that's just what I have been made to believe.* Maybe *that's not the truth at all.*

Maybe *beautiful moments are coming to find me.* Maybe *there is light around this corner.* Maybe *I will feel joy again.* Maybe *my life can be different.* Maybe *I do have a purpose and I can believe in my dreams again.* Maybe *I will heal.* Maybe *life will surprise me in glorious ways.*

Maybe *I am loveable.* Maybe *my life isn't over.* Maybe *I can find a way to breathe through all the suffocating moments.* Maybe *I am going to be OK.*

'Maybe' is the word that is the balancing point between two worlds: one, of your present or past reality, and two, of the fruitful possibilities that might be born through the different details constructing your reality right now. It is a beautiful and tender intermediary that allows you to acknowledge all the facets of what you are feeling and going through, without locking yourself only in them. 'Maybe' is like a foot that you keep out of the water, rather than being entirely immersed. It offers an axis for transition; to walk along a particular road and be attentive to stepping over onto a new road if and when it comes up. And what is so wonderful about this word is that it is tremendously honest. And, as we saw in Chapter 3, it is always helpful to be honest with yourself. There will never be a time in your life when it's better to not be honest with yourself.

There is a subtly empowering implication in 'maybe' that quite masterfully acknowledges the hardship and the struggle without getting lost in it. In any emotional or psychological healing, if you are going to walk the way that offers you as many restorative outcomes as possible, it's important to remain in touch with what you are genuinely going through. If you don't, you will bypass the processing of difficult feelings that need to come up and be aired so you can move on with your life. Sometimes an extreme reliance on positivity can get in the way of this. But 'maybe' offers steady ground to rest on while unearthing those difficult but necessary feelings. It can see the possible positives and it even beckons for them, but it accurately conveys the trepidation we often feel even when moving in that kind of direction. It honours the caution we take, even when we want good things for our lives. Rarely do we feel entirely confident to go in the direction of our dreams, even if we might tell the world around us we do. 'Maybe' allows us to stay real with the complexity of feeling that occurs when we are in transition from one landscape to another.

Sometimes our nervous system will shut down in order to protect our hearts from the overwhelming conditions surrounding us. The numbness tends to occur in protective reaction to any overwhelm evoked by difficulties. But 'maybe' offers a small way out of the intensity, making difficult feelings more bearable, so that you can actively participate in the work of acknowledging them and healing through the process. It offers an angle to take that you can't see when engulfed in heavy feelings. It is the middle ground between positivity and negativity, a reasonable space for us to settle in, so that we don't deny vast portions of ourselves because of an ideal of how we think we should live and deal with hard times. It is a gentle resting ground where you keep the flicker of hope alive, nurtured and growing in your heart as you wade through the circumstances.

The questions that pull me through the darkest of nights include, *'What else might be out there for me?'*, *'What else can I experience of myself?'* or *'What if everything does turn out OK?'* *'What if? What if? What if?'* These are a scaled down version of 'Everything is going to be OK' and continue in the power and opening of possibilities that 'maybe' generates. It's about looking out beyond your boundaries to see what else is there that you might not have picked up on. Those questions have the power to pull us through all the full stops we hide behind or feel imprisoned in:

> *What if there is more than this?*
> *What if there is more to experience of myself?*
> *Is there more joy?*
> *Is there more peace?*
> *Is there a way I can reach for new experiences and adventures;*
> *even new mountains to climb so that I can take in new scenery?*

Maybe there is. Seriously, just maybe there really is. And then the reflections continue to evolve . . .

Maybe this can change.

Maybe this moment can change.

Maybe I can find my way through.

Maybe the light is around the corner.

Maybe this will get easier.

Maybe brighter days are on their way, and they are going to
  find me.

'Maybe' is a very powerful heart and mind opener. Use it to keep your heart unfolding, to keep your mind inquisitive about new beginnings and how they might uniquely show up in your life every single time. Use it to keep your heart open in hope and in the belief in miracles, like when you feel like you're falling, but actually you realise you're learning to fly.

We are always conjuring up the worst possibilities for ourselves in our minds to try to pre-empt oncoming disasters. *What if* we turned it around? *What if* we used the same mind muscle to envision the best possibilities or at least some decent ones? It takes time. It takes effort to turn the pattern and habit around. But we get better at it as we put the time in. When I look at the mess with that question in mind, the '*What if*' question or the '*Maybe*' implication, verging towards positive outcomes, the opportunity to really consider that everything might be OK, through and despite the chaos, becomes more palpable.

These words fit very much into the category of self-support and learning how to mother your heart. They again formulate a wonderful antithesis to the inner critic that tends to pop up when facing harsh realities and sudden detours along the way. The spiral of unruly self-criticism that rears its ugly head with a vengeance when challenges occur is actually a crucial factor to affect your behaviour, sometimes even more than the difficult moment itself. You might find yourself wrestling with that most. Sometimes it's the way you tend to narrate how life feels for you right now, rather than objectively accounting the details, that imagines ruts in the road where there might not be. In the inspirational words of famous, gold-medal athlete Jesse Owens, 'The battles that count aren't the ones for gold medals. The struggles within yourself, the invisible, inevitable battles inside all of us, that's where it's at.'[1] So having these words and what they inform and imply in place, ready to cushion the blow of your negative automatic reactions and offer a way through them, can level out your vision and focus, so that the actual difficulties are easier to reframe.

SELF-REASSURANCE VERSUS SELF-ESTEEM

Over recent years, numerous studies have shown that engaging in self-reassurance, through practices, approaches and self-talk, can moderate the emotional and mental impact of adverse life events, even more so than the ways in which attributes of self-esteem feed the nervous system.[2] Self-esteem is based on how we see and value ourselves. It's like a subtle, personalised marking system, and your value tends to go up in your eyes when you prove to be successful at something. That, in essence, is how you develop self-confidence. On the other hand, you also wrestle with more feelings of shame, anxiety and disappointment because you tend to imagine your value going down when you fail. This yo-yo effect can create subtle and not-so-subtle pockets of tension in our responses to and interpretations of daily matters. Self-reassurance is a matter of mindset that get rids of all these measuring lines and, immersed in self-compassion, when setbacks and difficulties arise, it rushes to the threshold of that obstacle and pours a sense of care, concern, wisdom and perspective on the circumstance so that any struggle you go through is not punished with imagining a drop in your overall value. It gets quite technical if you have studied neuroscience or psychology, but, in layperson's terms, it is suggested that, when on the cusp of a difficult moment, it is even more helpful to say things like 'No matter what happens, everything is going to be OK', 'You will find a way', 'Even if you fall, you will get back on your feet' and so on, rather than 'I can do this', 'I will do this' or 'I am worthy of success in this.' That's not to say that the second set of statements are not helpful, but in the face of challenging encounters, self-support trumps self-belief in protecting our senses and awareness from the consequences of self-criticism.

Statements that seek to compassionately reassure self in the face of setbacks, serious mistakes and disruptions to life have a pacifying effect on depressive tendencies and other negative thought-patterning. In effect, there are established and proven neurological benefits in self-compassion and leaning on practices to build our self-reassuring inclinations in the face of the Great Mess. Learning how to talk to yourself with kindness and in a way that you do not deny the complexity of feeling you might be holding, while still nurturing faith in hopeful and positive outcomes, cannot and will not let you down. In fact, it can awaken a new kind of existence for you, one that is kinder on your nervous system and nourishment for your dreams, and all the faculties you need to make those dreams a reality. Even in the rare moments when the worst-case scenarios do eventually occur, despite your approach of self-kindness and emotionally integrated and hopeful filtering, you still won't regret the choice to pursue the positive outcomes that could have come out of the circumstance with honesty and hope in your pocket.

Write it out

1. Consider some of the hardest obstacles you are facing now and what you quietly or not so quietly fear about the possible outcomes. Try to use 'Maybe', 'What if' and 'What else' to offer a different perspective on them.

2. Have you ever experienced a hard time that has turned around to become something different from what you were expecting? Write about how life surprised you that time.

3. What can self-kindness replace in your backpack? And do you have any old expressions that you have often used that now feel outdated and unhelpful to you, as you look to expand your library of words? What can the words 'exhale', 'unrush' and 'maybe' replace?

CHAPTER ELEVEN

The Art of Balance

I have been looking for balance since my early thirties, after surviving three decades of extremes. In any extreme, you are always tipping over the edge of some kind of cliff. There is no positive extreme in my experience. Even the best parts of life when imbalanced are no longer the best parts of life. Even too much bliss is simply that; too much for your optimal sense of well-being, in the same way that eating too many sweets leaves you feeling sick and regretful of your indulgence.

ONE FOOT IN AND ONE FOOT OUT

I always suggest my 'one foot in and one foot out' technique when trying to ascertain a sense of balance as you wade through the challenges of establishing new principles in your life. It is also a wonderful way to look after your heart, mind and body when in the middle of some kind of upheaval or trouble. It's another tool to put in your backpack as you venture off into turning the Great Mess into a meaningful passage of growth and self-exploration.

I define 'being present' as having one foot in our inner world and one foot in the world around us. This is what having both feet firmly planted in real life looks like to me. It's also how I would define living with an open heart. It's when the two worlds that make up our existence dance together and we become conscious of how they boundlessly orbit around each other. Let me explain.

The inner life of a human being is a universe in itself. It is the conceptual landscape of our feelings, thoughts and sense of self, and all other energy that exists within us and through us. It is the realm of the sixth sense. It is where and how we feel love, anger, wonder, joy, chaos, sorrow, curiosity and fear. It is where we deposit our memories and extract meaning and feeling from them. It is the landscape of our consciousness, where our awareness of who we are can and does unfold. It is where the first-person narrator's voice of our personal stories is formed and resides, and where our subjective perceptions thrive. It is the playground of our imagination and the soil in which our deepest dreams can be conceived. It is who you are.

It is also where the destructive self-chatter belonging to that pesky inner critic has a field day, every day, until you learn how to hush it. It's where our fears can grip us from taking steps forward. It's where we overplay scenes and events from the external world over and over again. Sometimes we distort them. Sometimes we clarify them. Yes, sometimes, our inner world showcases what we are *and* what we are not.

The external world is a combination of our natural and social environment, and all its movement and activity. It includes the practical needs we aim to meet every day. It comprises the responsibilities we hold and how we carry ourselves. It also includes our physical existence, the health and ill health of our bodies and our physical interaction with the world around us. It is all the elements that make up the part of our lives literally outside of ourselves. Our external worlds are also us. And sometimes they are not.

We all tend to feel more comfortable in one than the other, but both worlds are indisputably connected and dependent on each other, creating equilibrium together. To develop and sustain optimal emotional health, you need a strong footing in both. Being connected to both parts of your life and approaching them like two halves of a whole is essential to being present in this world and growing a wholesome and holistic awareness of everything that makes you who you are.

We are defined by the states of consciousness we live in and our behaviour. We are made up of our unfulfilled dreams and our existing responsibilities. We are both our imaginings and the character we forge in our reality. To live with one foot in each generates a steadiness we can become comfortable, determined and confident in, especially when the ground beneath gets shaky and life suddenly turns stormy. You have more reserves to lean on and a more competent map to turn to when navigating through difficult currents in either sphere of your life. For example, when you are going through an immense amount of inner turmoil or pressure, trying to deal with some difficulty or sudden chaos in your life, directing some of your attention to the everyday tasks you have can offer breathing space from the difficult terrain you now have to make passage across. It can widen your vision, so that it is not wholly absorbed into the one area of conflict in your life. This in itself can help steady your nerves and keep your mind open, rather than diving into some kind of survival mode that has you shut down and unavailable to possibilities.

I learnt this very thing through motherhood. Be grateful for the roles you can't suddenly turn off or hide away from when in the midst of an internal storm, because, quite unexpectedly, they can offer you the anchor, distraction/focus and relief you need. Feelings can be frightening spheres of consciousness when they have enough room to sweep you away and control your actions. But when you fulfil at least some or even one of those tasks and roles, despite the feelings that are raging inside you, you are slowly building a state of mind based on equilibrium. Even something as small as getting out of bed and washing or brushing your teeth, when you feel like you have absolutely no motivation to do anything, helps to do this on a micro level. However micro it feels, it is still significant. That sense of equilibrium is a state of mind that will increasingly integrate your feelings rather than have you succumbing to them.

&

Feelings are there to be felt and to be felt through,
but not necessarily to be followed through on.

&

It works the same when overwhelmed with practical circumstances too. Taking time away and investing in other aspects of your life is a way to ease stress and worry caused by them. Rather than have your mind go around in circles over a work problem that is out of your hands until the following day, picking up the phone to talk to a friend or putting on some music and cooking up a wholesome meal for yourself offers you space away from the stress so that you can remind yourself that life is more than the problem.

It's imperative to actively remind ourselves that we have more going on in our lives than the struggles we are going through in the moment. We do it every week, with our working weeks and then our days off. Directing our attention towards concepts that illuminate and nourish the movements in our inner world and then actively investing in them, generates discoveries about yourself and life that the external circumstances have far less reach to influence. This is both empowering and restorative. In the face of unpayable bills, redundancy, abrupt changes, complications or endings in relationships, where it feels like all the tension and complexity of the overwhelming circumstances is mounting on top of you, taking time to physically look after your body and mind away from the heavy scenario can rejuvenate you and illuminate truths you couldn't tap into when seized by all your practical worries. Self-care can act as a magic wand. And finding balance is always a form of self-care.

VISUALISING BALANCE

I crafted a little visualisation based on the necessity of taking time-outs and why it's important to apply the principle of balance all through your days, all through your life, and definitely when you are facing some kind of demanding transition or disarray. Because of the sensory overload in such situations and how they tend to consume us emotionally, mentally and physiologically, it feels like there is no way out of them when they arise. They indeed take the driver's seat in our thought-life and often have too much influence on the subsequent choices we make. Practising walking away from the overwhelm through visual meditations slowly initiates new and expanded responses you can lean on in the future, when the overwhelm is fast approaching again. It's another way to give yourself permission — taking time-outs and balancing out where you are putting your focus can add significant empowering details to your perspective, and a subsequent sense of autonomy to break the cycle of regularly feeling intimidated and overcome.

Below is my visual meditation. As you read it, feel free to add any details that make the scene more personal to you:

Imagine a beautiful landscape; the kind of environment that makes you happy, even just to envisage it. Give me a white-sanded, Sardinian beach with transparent sea any day. You may be more inclined to conjure up tall birch trees or even the great sequoia, or red, rocky mountains, or miles of white desert sands. Whatever environment has you mesmerised and naturally unwinding, build a picture of it. Using your senses as a guide, conjure up some colourful details. Think of what you might see, what you might smell, what you might feel. The grass underneath your feet, speckled with daisies and buttercups. A warm sea breeze blowing through your hair. The silver-kissed moon passing by you at the edge of the earth. Imagine anything and everything. There are no rules. This daydream can be both familiar and mythical at once. The unicorns can be running with the horses, and elephants can be flying with reindeer above your head. Whatever blesses your spirit, conjure up and weave away. Be as detailed and specific as you can. The more details you paint onto this canvas of sorts, the more vibrant this mind-scene will become.

Once you have set up your scene (and hopefully had some fun doing it), imagine there is a little hut in this beautiful scene. And this hut comprises of one simple room. In that room is a table and two chairs opposite one another. Now, this is where you will need your imagination to go up a gear. If you can, I want you to imagine a kind of being/form that represents something difficult and consuming in your present life. It might be depression or self-hatred. It might be conflict at work or the relentless demands of being a carer. It might be toxicity in a familial relationship. It might be childhood trauma. It might be the catastrophic impact of a mistake you have made. It might be imposter syndrome. It might be grief. It might be your anxiety. Again, it can be anything

— whatever might be eating you up at the moment or does so on a regular basis. It's the thing you find yourself thinking about at night when the world has gone to sleep and it's also there waiting for you when you wake in the morning.

I tend to just imagine an outline for its appearance and then fill it with squiggles, or I imagine a huge ball of electric, bustling energy that can either grow or diminish, depending on the circumstances. Some people I have done this visualisation work with will imagine an actual person. It might even be someone they know and, of course, someone they deeply struggle with. But what's important is that you imagine it, sitting on one chair and you sitting on the other. You are facing each other and you are engaged together.

You don't have to be talking to one another, but there is some kind of communication, verbal or non-verbal, going on. It might just be an active, tangible awareness of each other and, whether your imagined being has eyes or not, you are interlocked in focus on one another, together. Visualise this for a couple more minutes. Imagine the feelings that normally arise when your attention is consumed with this particular issue or challenge. Make this essential stare-down as physiological as possible. You might imagine yourself sweating a little, or your stomach churning, or perhaps just feeling anger and frustration surge through your body. And at the point where your senses and thoughts feel as overwhelming as they can be, I want you to do something deliberate and purposeful. I want you to imagine yourself getting up from your chair, perhaps nodding your head at the abstract being in polite acknowledgement. But you turn around and walk away, leaving the table, the being and the room behind you.

You walk onto the veranda and you look out to the beautiful scene you have already created. You take some deep breaths. You

listen in to the bird song and feel the sun warmly kiss your brow.
You might venture out and walk along the tide of the sea, dancing
with the sand. You may sit under a tall tree and listen to the song
of the wind playing upon the leaves like hands on the black and
white notes of a piano. You may find your favourite cold drink
magically appears and you take some thirsty gulps of that.
(Everything is possible in the world of your imagination.)
Whatever it is you find yourself doing, you are allowed to do. You
get to walk away from the stress, the sorrow, the pain, the discon-
tent, the upheaval, the dejection and rejection whenever you need
to – whenever it feels timely or beneficial to remember other parts
of your life, other elements to your existence and indeed how you
experience your own self. Yes, you get to walk away.

Walking away doesn't mean leaving for good. Walking away doesn't
mean giving up. Walking away doesn't mean you are weak or incapable. It simply indicates it is time to recharge so you can power yourself up to go back and face whatever you need to face, once you feel
re-energised. Walking away means you step back so that you can
remember and notice more of life than this particular difficulty – the
beauty, the aliveness, the hope. Walking away makes you available to
new insight and perspective that you cannot access when something
is right up close and obstructing everything else. It reminds you that
you get to call the shots, more than you tend to think. It also opens up
an opportunity for you to again experience other aspects and expressions of who you are; the you who is also buoyant, fun, wild and
relaxed. Making contact with those parts of you when navigating
through chapters that are simply hard going is essential.

You might need to remind yourself of this time and again in any
messy situation. You might need to practise this visualisation over

and over again. But the message is simple and powerful: you can have one foot in the mess and one foot in life outside the mess, and actually that will offer you the balance you need to make your way through the obstacles and trials with your emotional and mental health intact.

∽

Just because the situation is messy, it doesn't mean that
it has to consume your entire waking and sleeping life.

∽

I remember sharing this particular visualisation during one of my live journaling workshops on Facebook during the lockdowns that took place all over the world in the Covid-19 pandemic. It received a lot of positive feedback. It was an almost revolutionary possibility – the idea that just because life is disconcerting and utterly challenging right now, doesn't mean you have to be plugged into the severity of it all the time. I kept repeating the words: '*You get to walk away. You get to notice something else. You get to experience something other than this. Your entire life is more than this moment. Just give yourself permission to move away from its grip for a little while.*'

It was a timely message, offering a forgotten possibility in the midst of a pandemic that had locked down our world, consumed all news outlets, conversations and the logistics for making everyday choices. I could read light bulbs going off for people in the comments underneath my live recording, as they practised the visualisation.

'Even with something as consuming and overwhelming as the pandemic, I get to walk away for a while?'

My answer was 'yes'.

Maybe not literally, because, for some, leaving the home was patrolled, but you get to walk away from the drama in your mind, and you always have the power to make small autonomous choices for your own benefit, no matter what you face. You don't have to watch the news. You don't have to keep up to date with the pandemonium we call social media (that was a big one for me). You get to have a break whenever you need it. What the break actually looks like is dependent on your circumstances, but you can always activate the mindset of the exhale whenever you need to (see page 129).

FEELINGS ARE MESSENGERS

One woman participated in that particular live workshop and found it so useful she got in touch with me after. She shared with me how overwhelmingly hard she had found the lockdown, because she was used to keeping herself busy. She realised that her efforts to keep herself occupied were actually a survival method she'd adopted many years ago, to keep her inner demons at bay. In the absence of the normal structure of her life, old memories of childhood trauma started to haunt her through the empty lockdown nights and days. By the time she came across my workshop, she was riddled by them. She was stressed, because, up until this point, her reaction was to focus on how to get rid of them, how to essentially squeeze them back into whatever closet in her heart she had once buried them. And nothing she tried worked.

Her focus was on what to do with them and trying to find ways to stop them drowning her. Her goal was to make them change. But this is what the visualisation aims to correct: the assumption that all your attention should be given to whatever is stressing you out in this moment, especially when it's very serious. To consider that she could have a moment back where these emerging and relentless memories weren't the central focus of her day or vision was revolutionary. The visualisation offered her a bridge in that moment to dip her foot in different terrain, in a different feeling, in details that would stimulate, or better soothe, her senses in a new way. I just wanted to present an opportunity to remind her there was life outside of her spinning thoughts. Even if she couldn't get rid of them, or put them back in the closet they escaped from, or change them, she could still show them her back, for a while, until she felt strong enough to look at them again – even if it was just in her imagination. She didn't have to follow their lead every time they came to the surface.

The one foot in and one foot out principle is essentially about how to navigate through strong feelings and learn how to hold them in place, as they arise, in response to difficulties, and often to express something inside you. We can feel all the feelings in the world without feeling like we have to follow their lead. This is so important to know when facing the Great Mess, because life's messiness has a way of conjuring up stormy feelings. And if you know that they do not have the last say and that they are also temporary, this will then help you to not be swept away by their currents. With both feet in your feelings, which essentially implies you identify them as a part of you, rather than just an expression of emotion that wants to pass through, you will feel controlled by them, confused by them and in contention with them sometimes too. But they are best summarised as messengers. The 'one foot in and one foot out' principle is a way of moving through the feelings without them consuming your actions and overwhelming your sense of direction. Keeping one foot in the feelings means you offer enough of yourself to feel them and not deny their presence, so that they can, in effect, pass through you and help show you something. Because all feelings are temporary. All feelings are essentially passing through. But keeping one foot out of them means you protect your actions and responsibilities from being controlled by the feelings that can and often do come at full force. And your actions and responsibilities are an important and empowering part of your life. You can make your dreams come true through them.

Write it out

1. You get to walk away from life's messiness when you need to. You get to have breaks. You get to put the burden down for a while. Look back on a difficult time in your life when you didn't know this. How might it have felt to get through it if you had?

2. Make some plans to balance out the tensions in your life right now. Work out where a particular tension is coming from and how you can lean on the other side of your life and participate in activities that give you a break from the heaviness.

3. Do you find you are someone who is more engaged with their external life and world or with their internal life and world? What are the pros and cons of that?

CHAPTER TWELVE

Through the Eyes of a Child

It is fascinating to see how our perspective about messiness changes over our lifetimes. It's also a little sad. Messiness begins as an opportunity and opening for fun, exploration, discovery and development. But, as we get older and become socially aware of ourselves (self-conscious) and understand the possible implications of having a mess (responsibility and consequence), it soon becomes a threatening space and force in our lives, with a heavy hand of judgement and sense of failure constantly hanging over it. However, if we can learn to use it as a compass and a guide, rather than seeing it as an enemy that deserves expulsion from our lives at all costs, embracing the messiness becomes a deeply empowering act of acceptance, restoration and creativity.

∾

*There was a time when you didn't fear the Great Mess
and chaotic beauty was still beauty in your eyes.*

∾

Looking at any kind of mess through the eyes of a child will, more often than not, differ greatly from how an adult perceives it. A child is not expected to clean up the mess in the same way an adult responsible for them is. Because of that inherent role and expectation, we automatically perceive any kind of mess in the light of what the result of it might be – that it needs to be cleared or resolved in some way, and then whether we feel we are capable enough to do that. But through this lens, we often miss what we might learn and discover, feel and explore, through the very experience of the mess. The child processes it in the opposite way and therefore the mess is a portal into new experiences and adventures, perhaps new worlds even, which is why a child's eyes will light up at the tremendous sight and an adult's will roll.

I remember the summer's day when I started writing the introduction for this book years ago. I sat on my brown, weathered, leather footstool, with shapes of light coming through my little window behind the TV. I have enjoyed many afternoons on my own, just before sunset, watching miniscule strings of dust float amidst the yellow beams coming in from outside, as if the dust particles themselves have been chosen from the gods to conjure up a dance to wake up the world of fairies. This again was the same.

I remember being spellbound by golden, sun-kissed dust when I was a little girl. I witnessed and comprehended on some level that dust could be almost otherworldly through the right kind of window, crack and curtain. And why not, when we return to dust eventually in this life anyway? And there, in that moment, with the dust dancing about me, mesmerising me yet again, I realised I had found a beautiful metaphor for the mess in our lives. Through the right approach, the right perspective, the right crack in our hearts, maybe the Great Mess could have something otherworldly about it too. Just dust from one angle and, from another, prancing speckles of tangible magic, hidden messages and dances; particles trying to wake up inside of us a sense of deeper knowing and deeper settling, deeper peace in who we are and whatever is our life in the moment.

I will always remember a story my husband told me about my eldest daughter who was around four years old at the time. My husband and daughter went to the local supermarket and he was just about to buy a six-pack of beer bottles. He put it on the counter ready to pay for it when my daughter suddenly pushed the bottles off the counter and they smashed on the ground, hundreds of pieces of glass and drops of beer flying out everywhere. My husband was obviously immediately irate. His reaction was justified. Our daughter had purposefully done it. Her curiosity had got the better of her. He was annoyed because of the action, because she might have hurt herself, because there were lots of people around who could hurt themselves or would at least be inconvenienced by it. He also felt embarrassed that she had created such a mess.

After telling her off profusely, her then subsequently crying, apologising to those who worked there, and then finally leaving the shop and both calming down, our daughter confessed through these words, as they continued to talk about it, 'but Daddy, it was just so beautiful'. She was talking about the mess, the light hitting off the shattered glass on the floor, the beer spilt everywhere. She was talking about her mind's eye before she even touched the bottles, that she imagined something wonderful to happen because of her actions and it kind of did, in her world anyway. It was dangerous. It was an inconvenience. But through the eyes of a child, it was also beautiful and fascinating. My husband still mentions that story to this day. It stopped him in his tracks at the time. He understood in that moment the allure of beauty; the innocence in curiosity, the impact of shifting perspective, how each angle is noteworthy in order to paint a complete picture. How the beauty and freedom created in mess can sometimes leave a longer-lasting impression than any temporary inconvenience or sense of jeopardy.

A child doesn't yet recoil at the sight of mess, because they haven't learnt it is 'wrong' yet. They are curious and sometimes delighted, whereas an adult often interprets a messy circumstance as punishment for something or a sign of some kind of failing. Adults shrink and turn away, whereas a child's interest grows and they get closer. The child has yet to identify messiness as an indication of some kind of personal or collective flaw. But through the processes of socialisation, they will eventually learn what we all do as we grow up: mess is wrong. Mess is scary. Stay away from it as much as you can.

∽

To really make friends with the Great Mess, we need to learn from children and get curious and ponder like we once did.

∽

The Great Mess is not necessarily an ominous threat, and neither should it be automatically treated like a punishment or attack of some kind. Instead, it offers you the opportunity to get close to some pieces in the mosaic of your life so that you can reposition them in a way that makes your life feel eventually more authentic and electric, reflecting the light inside you in a way that doesn't shun your darker aspects either. So that one day, you are taken aback, like my daughter was, by how those pieces glisten so beautifully in the sun.

Someone at some point told you that the mess of life was something that needed to be cleaned up and distanced from. But there is something in you that is older . . . the spirit of play, the essence of creativity, the wonder conjured up in curiosity and discovery. What if you approached the Great Mess with these elements as your guideposts? What if you replaced the resident and accompanying feelings of failure, judgement and mishap with play, creativity and curiosity? Can you imagine it? How you might exist through it? Would the mess feel, seem or appear different? You can succeed at this adventure of sorts, of turning around your relationship and perception of the Great Mess, because, once upon a time, approaching certain kinds of mess at least, wasn't something that would unsettle you. And that automatic connection you would make, where you would go forward in curiosity, with a hunch to find something fascinating, rather than turn away, is still there, somewhere, deeply buried inside of you. It is more you than it isn't, and that's a beautiful hope right now, if you can't accept it as a fact.

THE PROOF IS IN THE STORY

As much as I can, I try to get out in the garden with my youngest daughter every afternoon after nursery through the warmer months. I had her relatively late into my experience of motherhood and there are 10 years between her and my eldest. So, I have this recurring bout of mama-guilt, where I feel obliged to be as active with her as I was with my older two. It's a discipline that keeps my ageing body responsive to the demands of chasing after a now four-year-old. Although I would much prefer to sit around and just watch her play on her own, lemonade in hand and the sun's cheeky kiss flirting on my brow, she won't have that for a moment! She's my last child. And I don't want to miss a thing this time round. So, it's off on the trampoline we often go.

She is also definitely at that age where there is no limit to her imagination and there is no real order either. The stream of consciousness that flows through her when gripped in excitement and curiosity is quite impossible to follow if you are looking for something that follows a linear pattern. But throw that to the wind and you are in for the ride of your life. I am exaggerating, you still might find it all a bit silly, but, hopefully, you get my drift. Here's an example of how we got from a make-believe stable to outer space in about three minutes flat one afternoon:

I am suddenly a horse (because my little girl and her best friend were just playing 'horsies' at nursery). I get to run about on my feet but then I am asked to go on all fours so that she can climb on my back and I can carry her around (this is all acted out on our garden trampoline, by the way). I am not allowed to use English words. I am just to make horse sounds, so I do. She feeds me carrots, cucumber and hummus. Lots of hummus because that's what she likes, and she doesn't really ever have carrots and cucumber without it. She feeds me over and over again until my stomach is 'spilt'. I think she means that I feel sick because I have overeaten. Or maybe my tummy is split open for all the overeating – rarely does a child's imagination turn away from gore and bloodshed in make-believe scenarios! We go to sleep and then suddenly wake up because it's 'norning' (morning). But we wake up to see the moon discreetly perched in the sky. She is so excited to see the moon when the sky is still so light, that she starts screaming wildly, 'We can't reach you, moon. Our wings don't work.' The horsie game has suddenly disappeared. She is jumping and flapping her arms in earnest dismay, egging me on to join her. So I do. I can be a horse with wings that don't work. Why not? We both jump around, shaking our arms in a flurry, imagining that the harder we flap, the more the moon will beam us up upon it. Our wings still sadly don't work so then suddenly she brings in a rocket. And we are now on a rocket in space, but we still can't get to the moon. And then, suddenly, my girl instructs that we are now playing stuck-in-the-mud (a game of tag where you pretend to be stuck when you get tagged and someone has to go under your legs to 'unstick' you – and you need more than two people to play) as space dinosaurs! I can never quite work out how just the two of us can ever enjoy a successful game of stuck-in-the-mud . . . So, at this point, I'm really quite lost. It's all because of stuck-in-the-mud impracticality. We find ourselves caught in a magnetic orbit around some of the planets, but then my daughter freezes my wings so I can't use them again (this is definitely her taking over from my 'orbit' idea). I am no longer orbiting, but having my wings singed from then on, which I act out, imagining being hit by lightning every time my girl points at me and makes a shh sound to inform me her powers are working. The madness continues, much like how it started, until I get too tired, subsequently flopping on the trampoline, and return to being the horsie, wanting some more hummus – and sleep too!

Now, was that the ride of your life? No. But it sounded a little fun? Maybe. We can agree, though, that the narrative arc of those few minutes, confined to the imagination of my four-year-old, was disjointed and chaotic. In her eyes, it wasn't these things at all. I can imagine that the disordered storyline is a fair imitation of how she perceives the world right now. She is young and generally wholly dependent on her carers. I hold her hand and lead her. She goes with the flow of the day that is inclined to suddenly change direction at any given point. She has her routine, but it is loose and open to unexpected happenings – like space dinosaurs jumping out at us and chasing us back to earth during a rocket trip to the moon. She is noting these adventurous plots on TV and in storybooks every day, but they are outlined in a cohesive way. On a creative level, the consistency is obviously not important to her. She's captivated by the colourful detail of the experiences. That's what she remembers as she watches her many cartoons. And for her, I imagine it all connects. It's all life. It's all *her* life.

She thrived in our play together and had a whale of a time, also because she essentially felt safe. She was entirely familiar and comfortable with the objective setting, where she could launch into her imagination in any moment. Home is where she belongs, garden included. She was comfortable. She was with Mama.

In Jonathan Gottschall's very enjoyable *The Storytelling Animal*, he presents a strong and persuasive argument that the concept of story is at the very heart of the human experience. He proposes that stories are a profound and effective medium for sharing messages and observations. The realm of storytelling, that is as old as time, is an alternative world for the exploration of human experiences that you get to participate in, to a degree. And you don't have to leave your life or even your chair to do so.[1] But there is a fascinating (and almost obvious) detail that surrounds the kind of story we gravitate towards the most. We love a good story, no matter what the medium, that circulates around problems and crises. As an aspiring storyteller myself, I avidly agree:

'The idea that stories are about trouble is so commonplace as to verge on cliché. But the familiarity of this fact has numbed us to how strange it is . . . Stories the world over are almost always about people (or personified animals) with problems. The people want something badly – to survive, to win the girl or the boy, to find a lost child . . . The thornier the predicament faced by the hero, the more we like the story.'[2]

I think this undeniable correlation makes a lot of sense. Our love for this kind of story across the millennia is because the story arc constructed around misfortune, crisis and problem-solving is a loose and imaginative replica of our own experiences, tragedies and adventures through our lifetimes. We love stories that pivot around problems and challenges, because human life is full of problems and challenges. Stories reflect the emotions, cycles, digressions, traps, expeditions, battles, achievements, crises, escapades and quests that form together as the general framework of human experience. Stories are a mirror to our own struggles and breakthroughs. They are a guide, a confirmation, an exploration and a means of downloading and processing this intricate experience of life and death and everything in between.

So, this correlation is a powerful one. I take it as proof that the reason the storytelling art form has been established on relaying challenges, and basically whether or how the hero imaginatively overcomes them, is because life on this planet is founded on this particular aspect as well: the challenge and the breakthrough. In the same way that fish have adapted over time to better survive in their aquatic environments through colouring and streamlining in body shape, we are also dispositioned to assimilate challenges and struggles and overcome them as well.

Perhaps my little girl's apparent incoherence in our play session sheds further light on this. Maybe the fact that she jumps from one potential crisis to another in her imaginative play is because life can sometimes happen like that too. And at the point of her development – where she is safe and feels it, and her fundamental needs are entirely provided for – this causes no upset or confusion. She can indeed go with the flow of her sporadic imagination because that's exactly how she lives in her every day. She also finds some random way of solving the imagined conflict at each point. It might not make sense to my slightly worn-out and worn-down brain, but she is moving through and moving on from scene to scene, because she is already acclimatising to this world, full of challenges, highs, lows, triumphs, defeats and lots of beauty. She isn't guarded or closed off to the erratic nature of life. She doesn't feel threatened by it because she feels connected to her environment. And she has a lot of love around her as she does. I highlight these details because they have a significant impact on our ability, as adults, to surrender to the choppy nature of life.

In order to better flow with the frequent shifts in life, abrupt transitions that can feel like mini-earthquakes, avalanches and landslides, there are experiences, principles and practices you can put into place that will eventually evoke a similar kind of adaptability to the one my littlest so effortlessly puts on display, although in adult form:

1. *Locate and grow a sense of safety, assurance and steadfastness outside of the changeable variables.* Starving and moving away from the inner critic's toxicity is so crucial to that. I don't want to sound repetitive, but driving home this point is potentially life-changing. It's the barrage of aggressive criticism from inside of you that has you looking over your shoulder for bombs to go off more than anything else. That's what makes you feel homeless and like there is nowhere to rest your head. Once you learn to contain this negative force, you then start to give yourself permission to take breaks and find balance in the midst of turmoil. You walk into moments where you can find a place to stop and look out in awe of this life and this miraculous universe we are part of, and these moments balance the intensity of whatever chaos and mess you are also trying to make some headway in. You also start to clearly see the toxic circumstances, situations and relationships that you need to start walking away from (for good).

2. *Learn to feel safe by being open to actively nurturing loving and supportive relationships, where you feel loved for who you are and not just how well you perform and the things you do.* Become available to the possibility of having these kinds of connections with

people and put in the work required to do that. Sometimes that means declining from always dealing with problems on your own and actually asking for help.

3. *Step forward into the world.* Into responsibilities. Into showing up and showing up for yourself. Into relationships and sacred connections. Step forward into hard moments. It's in stepping forward to keep living that the process of healing can take place. It's in facing hard moments that we start developing the skill and capacity we are potentially capable of. We need to build up a collection of experiences that prove our anxieties and negative feedback loops wrong. The only way to do that is to take some risks and make yourself available to be surprised by life and what you can create by stepping forward into it.

4. *Get a better understanding of yourself.* This quietens the roars of the inner critic and it goes back to the power of honesty (see page 53). The way to deal with past traumas that have a strong grip over your present experiences and approaches to things is to unravel the deeper truths of all you have been through and understand what happened in the past in a holistic way. We begin to trust life again once we start exploring this sense of closure. Open up the corners in your soul that carry grief and let your feelings come up and listen to them, without letting them lead you astray into self-punitive rhetoric and behaviour. As you get more honest about what you feel and why you feel it, you will better understand yourself and therefore be able to integrate your experiences (even the messiest ones) into your selfhood, rather than living like you will never get out of feeling fractured and fragmented. There is more in this life for you. Getting therapy is an avenue to do this and journaling has been a wonderful tool for me to do this in my own life over the years.

THROUGH THE EYES OF A CHILD

5. *Choose curiosity over closing off.* Take the risk to be willing to be surprised, rather than assume you know how things will work out. Remember the words 'What if', 'What else' and 'Maybe'. They infer an open and interested outlook. Be willing to suspend your automatic 'doom and gloom' disposition and remember that chaos is the precipice in which to meet with many a dancing star.

Do you see how these principles loop in and out of each other? They are all indelibly connected and they bolster one another. If you work on one of these principles and practices, the connective elements in the neighbouring principles are also nurtured to support you as you experiment with surrendering to the twists and turns of life that the Great Mess has a habit of bringing to your doorstep in the form of crises and setbacks.

Write it out

1. Can you remember a time in your childhood when you experienced something like my eldest daughter did with the shattered glass? Do you remember when you first learnt that messiness was wrong or bad for you?
2. Think about something that really gets to you when it goes wrong. Is there a way you can approach it and perceive it so that you can track any prospects of creativity, growth and beauty in it for you?
3. More than anything else in this world, I think we want to be assured we are safe and to feel like we can handle life. Read the suggestions below and tick those you can relate to and already feel you enjoy in your life and then reflect and write

about those you would like to develop and how you can help make that happen. What feelings do these suggestions conjure up in you? Can you add to either list?

To feel like we are safe:

- Safe to live.
- Safe to leave our homes when we want to and go about our lives.
- Safe for our children to go to school.
- Safe to work.
- Safe to give following our dreams a good try.
- Safe to be who we are and explore ourselves.
- Safe to show our love.
- Safe in our bodies and in our significant relationships.

To feel like we can handle life:

- To own that feeling of handling life in our very bones.
- To demonstrate it to those we love.
- To strut it in the faces of those who always doubted us.
- To know we will stand tall in times of uncertainty.
- To lean on our resilience even when the horizon is covered over in fog.
- To assert a resounding 'yes' to life every time something beautiful is in the air.
- To roar a firm 'no' to the winds that threaten to destroy us as they blow against our dreams and the significance of our days.
- To always make something from whatever we have in our hands.

CHAPTER THIRTEEN

Acknowledge Your
Strength and Value

As children we display a keen interest in how to overcome challenges, manage catastrophes and survive disasters. I think this
is because, on a subconscious and conscious level, we pick up from a
very young age that a significant proportion of life loosely functions
in the same way. But even more than that, the sporadic and choppy
method of play highlighted in the last chapter – and characteristic in
mostly all young, budding imaginations/minds – could further
suggest that we as humans are also already emotionally and prag-
matically wired for the messy and erratic way life tends to transpire,
at seed-form level. And that's why we are comparably so durable and
have a good track record of surviving hard times. We are creatively
responsive and have this capacity brewing cognitively inside our
brains from our earliest years. But we don't tend to appreciate this
about ourselves, just like fish will only realise they are in water when
taken out of their natural environment, because they are too absorbed
in being in the water up to that point.[1]

So how can we get around this default dilemma of appreciation-
lack? It begins with acknowledgement: learning to acknowledge our

lives, and the grit and determination we already show, much in the same way that children are so well-disposed to do.

∽

You are more cognitively suited to deal with the Great Mess than you think.

∽

You will be surprised, more often than not, when you allow yourself to recount the potholes you get around in your life over and over again. You just have got so used to doing it that it doesn't feel like a big deal anymore. But *it is a big deal*.

Children get this. They do this so well. They acknowledge the things they accomplish no matter how small they might seem to the world around them. My daughter will show me the movements she has learnt at ballet every Wednesday. Hand on my heart, my daughter is showing me the same step over and over again, week in and week out. But to her, it's new. To her, she has achieved something once again. To her, it deserves to be noted by the world. My 'wow' is definitely mechanical, enthused with a near-genuine passion for everything she shows me. But that doesn't matter to her. She is different from the week before. Maybe she can hold her balance for a second or two more than she could last week. It is still worthy of acknowledgement, even if my old eyes can't decipher it. I have always wondered if this has even an inch to do with why a child will learn more in their first seven years than any other time in their life. The constant, self-perpetuating, positive feedback loop is inspirational, and I believe revolutionary. It's a radical loss when we stop doing this, and a life-changing rediscovery when we consider it as something to start up again.

Acknowledgement is the beginning of connection and possibility in every sense of the word. If you approached all the avenues of mess in your life as someone who is well-accustomed to making it through and conquering, imagine how much that might change your experience. You can meet your challenges because you are cognitively wired to excel through them. Now, that is a wonderful reconceptualisation of the Great Mess and your relationship with it to consider and play with.

It is reasonable to propose that, regardless of how your life might look on the surface to passers-by, on a personal level, days are tougher than they are easy. Maybe that is an understatement. Maybe that fact is so obvious. Life is demanding. Life is stretching. Life will push and pull you along. You will feel dragged and thrown about. You will contend with forces that are way out of your scope of experience. It is the constant struggle between beauty and tragedy; meaning and foolishness; mistake and mastery; impulse and responsibility; ignorance and awareness; success and failure; projection and objective reality. And it is a struggle that happens every day, in a variety of ways.

Let's list some of the subjective elements that make life on a daily basis a difficult thing to manage. In no particular order, these are:

1. Monkey mind: when your mind is vaulting from thought to thought in an escalated way, keeping you preoccupied with worries and confused thinking, so that you can't focus on the present moment.

2. Negative feedback loops: where you can't work out whether your anxiety is directing your observations or your observations are giving cause for your anxiety to rise. But you suffer from symptoms of panic of different degrees that can be both physical and emotional, and feel directly detrimental to your mental health and sense of well-being. They can leave you

feeling isolated and estranged from your own self, people you love and the world around you.

3. The fear and reality of being judged and misunderstood by the world around you and how that uniquely shows up day in and day out.

4. Childhood trauma triggers that create a sense of being stuck in a claustrophobic maze that you can't find a way out of. We tend to take our subsequent frustration from being on the receiving end of them out on ourselves and others. And old, unhealed wounds erupt, seemingly out of nowhere.

5. The inner critic and all the syndromes that come with that: low self-belief, imposter syndrome, strong social anxiety.

6. Suffocating and overwhelming emotions you wade through, like depressive cycles and post-traumatic stress disorder.

7. Collective anxieties, instability and competing narratives on a community, national and global scale that are manipulated and excessively communicated through the media (social, news and advertising).

8. Grief and the complexities and frailty of human relationships.

9. Problems with your health. Problems that have been misdiagnosed or have been left without a name, and it's a struggle to gather any real understanding over why your body is behaving like it is.

10. The constantly prevalent practical stresses, such as not having enough money, not having enough time in the day to get everything done, having to wear so many hats and dealing with family drama and difficulty.

Take a breath with me. I don't want to overwhelm you, but the list could be even longer. I am sure you could add many things to it. You might see a mother kiss her daughter before she gets out of the car. What you do not see or hear is that they have just had a conversation about putting a support and safety plan into place so that the cyber-bullying the girl is presently victim to can be addressed and stopped. You might see two men laughing heartily together in the street. One of them returns home to punch the mirror in his hallway because he hates being alone, he hates himself and he feels inferior and resentful towards the guy he was just laughing with.

Life is tough. And yet, every day you get through all of that, to wake up to the sun dawning on the horizon once again, and to give this thing called life all you have in the tank, once again. The amount of struggle changes day to day, but there you are trying, with all the odds listed above seemingly working against you. That's why it is not a falsity when you read quotes that remind you of how strong you are, that you are more capable than you realise. You prove it every day, despite the struggling, the crawling, the limping, the recalibrating. One of the dictionary meanings for 'strength' is:

> (n.) The capacity of an object or substance to withstand great force or pressure.

If you look up synonyms for 'withstand', you will find words like 'cope', 'ride out', 'suffer', 'endure' and 'survive'. So, strength is the ability to cope, to suffer, to ride out, to endure and to survive. But what we tend to conjure up in our minds when thinking about strength is the impression that we should be walking around, oozing ultra-confidence, stability and a kind of invincibility too.

This might be a platitude. You might have heard this and read this a thousand times before. But . . . you are stronger than you think. Significantly, though, there is something that is even more profound than that: you are stronger than you *feel*. And that is a disconnect we are constantly duped and weakened by, until we decide to do something about it.

THE COST OF SENTIENCE

Humans are highly sentient – feeling – beings. The feelings we carry have a considerable impact on our choices, our perspective, our actions and all we secretly believe about ourselves. This is why it's so imperative and empowering to learn how to hold big feelings in place and not have them control us instead. But because we *don't feel* what we prove to be and demonstrate on a daily basis, we struggle to believe we are that very thing. There are many incredible perks to being intrinsically sentient. Our very existence is a voyage through dimensions of solid reality, full of encounters steered by abstract concepts that we cannot touch, hear, smell or see, and yet we feel them and know them to be real. But this is perhaps one of the disadvantages of having such a dominant feeling gene. The fact that a noticeable proportion of what we feel doesn't always match up with particular facts about our character we so readily put on display is a significant drawback we have to learn to manage and supersede.

Let's use the attribute of strength to further illustrate this. When you don't feel like you are strong and yet you show a particular strength every day – through your commitment, your responsibilities and your resolve – you are still more likely to go along with the feeling and have it guide your ideas about yourself, rather than pay attention to the evidence. Because of this disconnection, it makes it impossible to really own that strength, wholesomely identify with it and employ it in a way that we can best benefit.

To own your strength, you have to begin acknowledging where

you have shown strength. In doing this, a new realm of experience opens up and instead of your wayward feelings always leading the way, they start to gradually line up with the evidential truth – the grit and determination you show each day. As you begin to acknowledge these points of truth, your feelings will respond and transmute because of all you are recognising over time. Your spectrum of feeling not only expands but rewires itself. And the feelings that have dominated your opinions about yourself and have left you in conflict up until now become diluted with this new concentration on the truth. And then your strength becomes compounded – through the combination of demonstration *and* subsequent sensation as your feelings start to reflect what you demonstrate day in and day out.

It's through acknowledgement that our spectrum of feeling remoulds itself to be more accurate and reflective of the truth over time. Our feelings become responsive to what we focus on with intention and purpose. So, if we are always focusing on all that we are yet to accomplish or produce, our feelings will mirror the sense of lack we keep on noticing, rather than any skill and ability we already possess. Focusing on lack makes us feel we are lacking (as we briefly touched on in Part One through the deficit mindset, page 34). And if you do that, then *feeling* strong is almost impossible, despite the strength you show every day.

YOU ARE STRONGER THAN YOU THINK

When you hear someone confess to being tired of being strong (and that has been me many times), I think what is really trying to be communicated is that the person is tired of doing hard things and getting through those hard moments, without feeling the strength they display as they do it. It's not that we get tired of being strong; we get tired of not feeling strong, because it feels wonderful when we get a sense of this strength in our own subjective processing. When we break down a door that has kept us encaged, when we reach a milestone, when we push through a limitation, when we surprise ourselves, when we step forward to a challenge rather than hiding away . . . When this kind of resilience is acknowledged to the point that it is physicalised in our body through feeling and sensation, there is not much else that feels more electric. So, feeling strong is riveting. It is invigorating. And we want to feel more alive. It's just that living day to day often seems like a draining undertaking when we don't feel strong. And we can change this. We can feel it more, because we demonstrate it more than we give ourselves credit for. If we felt it more, meeting the difficult moments in our lives wouldn't feel so soul-destroying. You are strong. There is no doubt about that. But now it's time to feel it.

You deserve to feel all that you are. I don't doubt you feel and own your flaws. We are so good at picking apart our weaknesses. But you deserve to extract all the goodness you can from your strengths and personally experience them in your senses, in the same way you might experience your anxieties or your self-doubt. Your weaknesses make you feel weak but your strengths don't make you feel strong. This is the sizeable disequilibrium that we need to set ourselves the task of rebalancing. You need to learn to extract all the nutrients in the positive demonstrations of your character and they will fuel you to continue along your path with vigour and purpose, despite what the Great Mess might bring to your doorstep.

∽

You have enough in your hands to begin weaving
up the miracle you are looking for.

∽

DEVELOPING A POSITIVE GAINS MINDSET

You need challenges to occur to give you the opportunity to demonstrate what you are made of. Those challenges can prove you have the strength you so want to connect with and own in a new way. But if you don't acknowledge the hard things you do, you will feel like a fly in a jar. It seems like the canvas of your life is yours to fly in, explore and call home, but you can never actually access those possibilities. You won't be able to connect with the strength you show in a tangible way and eventually you may come to resent that particular aspect of yourself and life for being so difficult all the time.

You need to stop taking for granted the way you pick yourself up time and time again and instead place value on it with grace and a propensity to grow. We tend to bow out early in any exchange with the Great Mess because we don't respect how far we have come and what we have achieved along the way. We tend to either overindulge in it to mask all the debilitating self-doubt we harbour deep down or totally dismiss it because of that stronghold of self-doubt.

We find it easier to focus on what we need, what we're missing, what doesn't add up in our lives. And we don't see enough of what we have. This isn't a call to gratitude – this is a call to balance, because this is partly what leaves us feeling ill-equipped, intimidated and weak in the face of challenge.

You need to bring to the surface of your memory the good you have in you. You need to be daring enough to acknowledge beautiful things about you, to stand up and sing your praises when they're due. It's partly how you level things up with the Great Mess. It's how you get on an equal footing with it. It's how you get into position to see the bright details in the horizon up ahead and allow your heart to do its bit and lead you there, with your mind following rather than hindering. It's how we grow an awareness of our innate worth. This is how we keep or get our heart open. When we stop peering out to the world from a place of lack and instead commit to nurturing an awareness of what we have inside us and what we have in our life, the world around us looks different. The Great Mess looks different. The obstacles become approachable. Our hearts feel softer and our spirits stronger. The menacing threat of what hardships might bring slowly reduces, because our awareness is focused on other details.

∽

You can do hard things because you are already doing them, even though you might not feel like you are.

∽

The real challenge, beyond whatever it is you are facing, is to realign your ideas about yourself from the point of considering you have enough inside you to deal with the challenges, or at least, you have enough potential to do it. I call this a *positive gains mindset* (the antithesis to the deficit mindset mentioned on page 34). It is something you don't have to immediately agree with, but please at least ponder on it. When we make the commitment to begin meeting each day from a mindset of gain rather than lack, it can feel daunting at the start. It's like you are turning your world the other way round. But, it is so worth all the effort required. When you face the world with a 'gain mindset' – when your focus is on all you have inside you, when you want to grow and develop, rather than giving premise to that age-old narrative of never having or being enough – what you are essentially asserting and making your way towards is the superlative truth that *the world gains on this very day because you are in it.* It bears repeating here, that to face life consistently from a place of being swarmed in feelings of deficiency, the message that is sent out to the world from that stance is basically saying '*You are lacking something today because of me.*' And this couldn't be further from the truth! But that stance is a black hole. All the good practices that you develop, on top of that fundamental position of feeling inadequate, can disappear into that void at any time.

And that's why it's necessary to strip back to its core the kind of dialogue we tend to have with ourselves, so that we can become conscious of any damaging untruths we are unintentionally feeding into and then consciously move away from them. You are not undervaluing your losses and the absences in your life that have made you feel deficient when you do this, but – and this is the key – you are no longer solely defining yourself by them. Living from a gain mindset is revolutionary because you are actively feeding into the truth that you are of value in this world. You are placing yourself in a position of strength. Imagine the details you might notice of the Great Mess if you approached it from a position of strength and enough-ness. It's like noting a mountain you are about to climb and not getting fixated on how difficult the trek might be, but instead being inspired and intrigued by the sights you might find, the new memories you will create and the challenges you will overcome and prove your ability through.

It was a real turning point in my life when I realised I wanted to experience more of myself than just share who I was with the world every day. I didn't just want to be strong and offer that support as strength to others; I wanted to *feel* strong, so that I could enjoy some of the attribute too. I wanted to walk around like the strong person that everyone could feel I was. I was tired of quietly feeling the opposite inside me – inferior, intimidated and doubtful all the time. After being able to put into words this imbalance I had felt for many years, I got to work on changing this, so I didn't feel left out in all I was in the world. These habits need time to mature and become integrated into your default perspective on life so that you have truths fully activated inside you to lean on when the time calls.

Write it out

1. Create a list of some of the things you have proven yourself to be over the years and note if you feel the sensations associated with those attributes. You might look back over your life and find that you have proven yourself to be resourceful, loving, steadfast, loyal, open-minded, courageous, generous, and so on.

2. Do you know what those aspects of your character feel like in yourself? This is not about how you make other people feel, but how it feels to be that kind of a person, full stop. If you do, write about what those attributes feel like for you. How do they inform how you see the world? What do they give back to you? If you don't know how they feel, really take some time to acknowledge the times you have demonstrated those aspects and imagine what people have felt around you. For example, if you are a warm person, but you feel quite cold-natured towards yourself, imagine what life would feel like if you were warm to yourself in the same way you are to others. It could be that you are helpful and caring, but you don't feel helpful and caring towards yourself . . . Build up an impression of what the feeling is behind the being.

3. When was the last time you felt like you were enough? (Just write whatever comes to mind, even if it's 'never'. Start from there and see where you go.) Feeling like you are enough is something you want to bring in your backpack and lean on in times of difficulty, so let's look at a journaling exercise that will help you to grow that sense of self-assurance in yourself. Imagine yourself feeling like you are able, strong and brave.

How would that change the way you talk to and about yourself? How would that change the choices you make, the things you notice about your life and how you would carry yourself? Finish this reflection with these words: 'The world is a better place, because of me' and then write out whatever comes up in your heart as you ponder those words. Be as honest as you can. Remember, you are not trying to write the right thing, you are just trying to offer your deeper thoughts and feelings an outlet, so that you can connect with them and comprehend them even better.

The madness we can dance with.

The brokenness we can create with.

The rejection we can transform with.

The shattering we can soften with.

The sorrow we can make friends with.

The truth we can be brave with.

The healing we can be inspired with.

The worthiness of our souls, we can make peace with.[2]

PART THREE

When in the Mess

We have thoroughly explored what to do when making your way through the terrain of the Great Mess, how to meet it when it appears and why you can move forward through it. Now with the essential guidelines in place and your backpack packed, you are ready to begin your expedition of transforming your experiences with the Great Mess, so that you come out feeling empowered by the exchanges, rather than defeated. This stage, in itself, will commence a whole new period of self-discovery for you. Be excited. You will surprise yourself. And you will pass through any upcoming tests and challenges because your heart – the very source of your power – is opening and you will learn to tailor all you have learnt to the environment. Remember this also: the human spirit has an uncanny propensity to turn what's ugly into something beautiful or at least artful, and to transform something utterly tragic into an expression of hope, even when it's not required or encouraged. *That* is the spirit inside you.

Imagine this section like a brief travel guide about some exclusive signposts to look out for, that will offer both guidance and confirmation, and also do the trick of keeping you on the right path in moments of uncertainty and discouragement. These last chapters explore how to better interpret the difficulties in the transformative journey that lies ahead. As you venture out into the Great Mess – the world of circumstances and obstacles that have made you feel inferior up to now – be prepared to find wisdom and companionship in the most unlikely places. You might step up to slay monsters and then realise they are helpers in disguise. You might find bridges that crumble as you walk on them, so that you are not pulled away from the quest at hand. You might climb mountains that were once thrones to giants, only to wake up the giant inside you. At some point, the rite of passage begins to highlight not so much what you find along the path, but how the quest itself helps you to understand yourself better, access deeper peace and utilise your inherent power more than ever before.

Now is your time to further formulate the legend that is your life.

CHAPTER FOURTEEN

Listen In for the Stories

For as long as I can remember, I have always wrestled with the traditional composition of 'purpose'. It's the idea that we are alive today to fulfil some kind of calling on our lives. It's been a problem ground for me, as I have watched it motivate extreme approaches to life in different degrees, including my own. My dogmatic interpretations of purpose had me thinking for too many years that whatever I was here to do took priority over who I was or, more importantly, how I was doing. I got trapped in a framework of thought that prioritised my service and performance over my well-being. Through it, I essentially endured over a decade of treating myself almost like a slot machine. I didn't consider the concept of recharging. I wasn't really concerned with my well-being at all. It was all about my performance – which translated as overworking, not slowing down, constantly focusing on the goal at hand . . . Everything I did for myself was about how much it would help me perform better and race towards my dreams faster, rather than whether it was actually good for my emotional and mental health. To be honest, I didn't consider my mental and emotional health at the time at all. I had a purpose to fulfil and I would fulfil it at any cost.

It became my exclusive means for locating the validation I so sought. And the truth is, my ideas of purpose were steeped in my own personal wounds and excruciating insecurities. This, I only worked out in my thirties. We can use our 'purpose' as a way to keep the pain at bay and to stay distracted from getting honest with ourselves. So, my twenties were overwhelmed with all the energy I could conjure up to fulfil this 'purpose', because I really didn't want to face my pain and brokenness. It was an impression of purpose I pieced together, through my fractured sense of self and a lens on life that had cracked in my childhood, and I hadn't yet realised needing repairing. Singleheartedly chasing after my purpose, and the subsequent valida-tion I hoped to receive from that, eventually made me lousy in my self-care and self-love practices and, fatefully, in my relationships. It made my vision blinkered and I became a purpose snob. I only gave time and attention to whatever I thought might help propel me forwards into the vision I had for myself. It meant that the pressure was on me to always see accurately. I wasn't open to being surprised, learning and shedding old ideas. I was too scared to loosen my grip. And I became hideously self-absorbed. I finally collapsed beneath the pressure I put myself under. My relationships collapsed under the weight of neglect I had shown them. It was then that I started to chal-lenge the flat and linear version of purpose that had governed my life up until then. The truth is that I felt insignificant without a sense of special purpose. I realised I needed to feel worthy despite it.

THE LIBERATION IN STORY
I came out of this existential crisis replacing the significance of purpose with the value of story. This was another quiet revolution taking place in the corners of my consciousness. There is a strong

deterministic element to traditional ideas of purpose that offers stability. But it trades in nuance, creativity, mystique and unassuming curiosity for that certainty. It is comparably absent of human and cosmic artistry too. When everything is purposeful, there is a glaring component of predictability involved. But it is predictability that counters the possibility for creative magic which humans need in order to thrive. To really find true meaning in this world, we have to activate our own creative intelligence and participate in the way it randomly and deliberately manifests and dances between the patterns of our everyday lives. We have to be willing to remove the conclusions, take away the full stops and continue to unfold the mystery of being alive that, in itself, might not even be complete yet. As the universe continuously expands, so should our perspective.

The concept of story allows for this fusion of heightened awareness and any temporary friction it produces along the way, because it is a part of the creative process anyway. Mark Turner writes in *The Literary Mind* that, 'Narrative imagining – story – is the fundamental instrument of thought. Rational capacities depend upon it. It is our chief means of looking into the future, or predicting, of planning, and of explaining.'[1] It is a portal for language that facilitates a fluid responsiveness towards one's revisions of meaning, as the mind matures.

Hence, I dropped being so obsessed with fulfilling my purpose and the surface, stressful and oscillating experience it produced. I exchanged it for a story-focused approach. My nervous system was soon grateful for the switch. So was my family. Rather than consider the purpose of things, I started to look for the story in them instead. I wanted to find the stories being told, the stories that might be told, the stories that were still untold and the stories still waiting to be incubated.

The purpose in things is generally one-dimensional. It's a necessary thing to note, but if that's all you measure your life to, it can

become very restrictive. When you also note the story in something, you find yourself spotting an array of different details that
you might have looked past when just focusing on the purpose of
things. The story opens up dimensions of details and magnifies
your awareness of life. I applied the story-full approach across the
expanses of my life. For example, rather than focus on the purpose
of my mistakes, I leaned towards the story in them. It gave me
perspective enough to not be so quick to criticise and punish, but
find, forgive and reconnect with myself and build a more loving and
integrative internal dialogue, even as I took responsibility for my
actions. I learnt the hard way that you can be entirely engaged with
whatever you think your purpose is and, in the same breath, be
unaware and absent to other key and powerful details of your story
that offer your life nuance, substance and dimension, like your
character, and your relationships, and your setting (surrounding
environment of your every day) and so on.

Essentially, the story-full approach gave me room to breathe as it
evolved to be a gentler, more detailed and expansive sensibility – a
way of translating the world around me and how it spun on its axis
every day. Turning this approach towards the messy moments of life
is a game changer. It assists in finding ways to not take the happenings of life at face value. It opens the way to stick with the seeming
difficulty for enough time to see what might come of it, how it might
surprise you and how it might serve you.

∽

Breathe, darling. This is just a chapter;
it's not the whole story.

∽

There is a beautiful implication of continuance and fluidity in story-telling and creating that is a gift to any mind that tends to get fixated on details. It allows for trial and error, twists and turns, and passages into truths and understanding presently beyond our own. We meet moments like they are pages and seasons like they are chapters. The feeling is that there is always more. Not just more to do, but more to explore, more to learn, more to be surprised by. Ask any writer what the most difficult challenge in creating any story is and they will always admit it is finding a way to end the story, and deciding upon the right kind of ending, for that matter. Stories inspire us to love, to hope, to protest, to be human and to feel like we have less to lose, that not all is lost, as we do, because of the subtle promise that there is a tomorrow on its way, or another page, or another chapter. A story-full mindset promises a point of redemption in mistakes, turning points when we go off track and desperate inspiration when we hit rock bottom. The point is that we get to write the story from the point when we realise we can.

Our purpose is normally a way to define our lives with a reason for existing that has been determined before we have had any direct, conscious thought or interaction with it. The responsibility that falls on our lap is, therefore, not so much to create but to fulfil a kind of mission. The stakes are automatically higher. The expectations are more solidified, and the possibility of failure is denser than in the story-full approach. In the latter, I have found the opportunities to co-create with life and evolve as you do, to be vitalising. As Hannah Arendt wrote, 'storytelling reveals meaning without committing the error of defining it'.[2]

A STORY-FULL APPROACH

Storytelling works well when dealing with messy moments as well. If messy moments are just part of your story then the degree of finality you might have associated with them in the past, especially when you might have perceived them as an obstacle to you fulfilling your potential, is majorly reduced. When your life is not about where you reach but more about what you experience as you try to get there, it helps to moderate any coming turbulence – because you treat it like it is simply air pockets to move through, rather than the irrevocable threat you might have once presumed it to be. And life transforms to become predominantly about who you are and how you are, rather than just what you do. In fact, once you change the axis of your life, for all aspects of it (including the messy parts) to evolve around who you are and the story that is revealing you and the life you are exploring, a marriage between who you are and what you do takes place, and your life transitions to become wholly integrated, rather than the fragmented and fractured experience it has been for many years.

The key is to treat the messy parts of your life as components of your story or smaller stories in your grand story, rather than the potential force to destroy you. This way, you are more able to find the resolve you need to meet the challenges and use them for your benefit, if any can be found. This approach guides you to delve in deeper and explore what you can't find on the surface of things. Processing your life through the parameters of story-crafting allows space for scenes to develop and evolve, for scenery to expand and character development to ensue. The forecasts of finality are substituted for the unravelling of cosmic ingenuity and creative intuition. It's an exciting and incredible liberation to not know where you might end up and yet simultaneously feel like you are in the author's seat, writing away to reach wherever that might be. The beauty of the story element to your life is that in your choices, in your actions, in your perspective, in the stories you tell yourself and the ones created featuring you in them, you have the last word. You might not have a say in all of it, but the last word is always yours. May it become a word saturated in kindness. Once we really own this in our very bones, we can stand tall, rather than back off when life gets complicated.

On some level, everything is a walking story, and stories are everywhere, waking to themselves and then falling asleep all over again. The land has stories. The rivers collect stories. What is each ripple in the sea if it's not a tiny tale that is part of a far bigger one? Each petal budding on its flower holds a story in its silky cells. I have often wondered about all the stories that old trees have overheard through the decades of their life, as humans pass them by, gossiping, laughing or arguing with one another. And the billions of tales that have been spoken to the moon on a bright night. Each star in the sky flickers a tale and each sigh we exhale carries a piece of story in it. Why not then the messiness of life? Why does the Great Mess have to be something separate? Surely it can be depicted as a story? Surely it can be understood as a story or, like I once wrote, a chapter in a story, too?

∽

Look for the 'signposts' that point to a story being told.

∽

If there is a story being told, we are more likely to listen in, rather than run away. We are more likely to hone in on the details, rather than get lost in the blur of our minds. This is story's power! We are willing to suspend our disbelief (even in ourselves) readily, for the sake of plot and intrigue. When the messy aspects of life form just part of our story, the general story they are embedded in always takes precedence over any one aspect of it. Listen in for the story of the mess you are facing. Listen in for the potential of rebirth, growth, freedom and meaning you might find on the other side of the dilemma. The symbolism, the tone, the cliff-hangers, the hyperbole, the juxtapositions, the resolution. There is a story happening right now. And this moment in the story might hurt and your heart might ache, but this is the work of story too. Every good story will break your heart and leave you lost in the fires of life, demanding justice, change or truth at some point. When approaching the messy moments like this, it won't hit so hard when you see parts of your life as you know it shatter before your very eyes. It will hit like it should. It will make you feel entirely human. But at the end of your tears, it will also whisper of tomorrow. This is why the human spirit is a force in itself. We believe in the unfinished, in continuing, in the dawn that follows the night.

What hits hardest is when we imagine that there is no tomorrow. That there is no possibility for a turnaround. That there is no light that will meet the darkest night sky and say, 'That's your time done until the next.' The beauty of story is that, more often than not, it says there always is. There might be a hint of redemption or a comeback, or a strong promise of a sequel, or a new chapter, or the ending is left open because there is no real ending at all. Look at the mess of your life through the lens of storytelling and take the leap to realise you are not in the story of your mess, you are the author of your story, and the mess is part of your tale. You are the one who gets to narrate the story whenever you are ready. Through this approach, you can learn to make home in your evolving power.

THE LIMITS OF PURPOSE

Not everything has a purpose. And that's a really important point to remember for all of us who have a habit of overthinking and over-analysing. But most things do. I imagine the ratio of purpose to purposelessness in life to be similar to the yin-yang. That small circle in both parts is the space that purposelessness takes up in the world. They are small but significant. Acknowledging that some events and encounters that happen have no purpose offers a way to get through the most horrific ordeals. Sometimes crashes just happen. Sometimes you are in the wrong place. There is no greater good to be found in them. There is no remarkable metamorphosis promised through them either. Some things are just to be survived. The survival itself is the medal of honour. It is best advised to walk away from the mean-ingless crashes in your life, as soon as your emotions and processing will allow for that response.

∾

Always seek to put the pointless behind you.

∾

May you learn to look back on the difficult challenges, days, episodes and chapters in your life and trace signs of strength you weren't even aware you were embodying at the time. Let them feed into your epic story. May you be able to find glimmers of grace that kept your heart soft enough to stay open and keep you responding and creating. And may those new findings inform your current ideas of all the scenes in your life right now.

Write it out

1. What do you think your purpose is? Has your idea of it changed over the years? (It is totally fine if you don't know what your purpose is. I don't think in terms of purpose anymore, but I just want to create space for your own feelings on it.) Does it feel heavy? Does it feel meaningful?

2. What is your story so far? And what direction would you like your story to go in, in the future? What chapter do you feel you are in right now?

3. Think about a difficult thing in your life right now and try to tell the story of it, and tell the story of you dealing with it. Wherever you stop, go back to it in a day or two and add to the story of it.

CHAPTER FIFTEEN

Look Out for the Goo(d)

I have always wondered why we don't call the caterpillar and the butterfly a 'butterpillar' and a 'caterfly'. I write that sentence in jest, but the process and transitions of life in the cycle of this duo-being is entirely remarkable. And yet this wasn't the detail that drew me so much to butterflies, to the point that I would name my business in part after them. It was actually a lot simpler than that. I simply fell in love with how close they bring an ethereal beauty to our senses. How they make an alternative and seemingly faraway world feel like it's just on our doorstep. It's something about their movement, their shape, the direction they take. It's the fact that they are more wing than anything else and yet, ironically, they cannot see their wings. It's the way light travels through their thousands of tiny scales, reflecting photonically on each other to glitter in the sky above. The dance of the butterfly can lighten any heart that takes note of it.

It's quite remarkable that the beauty of the butterfly is the produce of the worst fear come upon the previous caterpillar. I like to think of it this way anyway. It is a symbol of hope for this very reason. Few creatures ever want to die when the time comes. The prospect of death is only ever appealing when another moment of life feels totally unliveable. Or you have so ascended both the suffering and the bliss associated with being alive, that when the post-death realm (whatever that looks like to you) comes knocking at your door, you wholly surrender and invite it in without much thought. You either have to be enclosed in pain and suffering, bled dry of any hope or, on the other side of the spectrum, inspiringly ascended and yielded to a transient, transcendent concept of life. And I note how inspiring the latter is because I can't imagine myself quietly surrendering to death.

I imagine the death of the caterpillar to be very different from how you might imagine an old Zen monk to bow out of life on this planet. But humour me. I have no scientific study or evidence to support my imaginings, just some wild, fun thoughts that I want to use to hopefully make a compelling point about how to interpret different details of any mess you might, at some point, find yourself in.

DEVASTATION IS NOT FINAL

I would argue that the caterpillar goes through two episodes of its worst fears:

1. This seemingly gluttonous eating machine actually faces the unthinkable: it runs out of food.
2. It can't help but feed on itself in response.

Imagine that for a moment: eating parts of your body and not being able to stop yourself from doing it because you are compelled, instinctively. And it's an instinct you cannot override because it's the basis for your life up to this point and indeed the particular variable to ensure your very future. And all you witness to emerge out of this seemingly ruthless trick in nature is yourself disappearing into a gross, gooey substance.

Now, obviously, I am succumbing to what the *Oxford English Dictionary* would call an innate human tendency – I am translating a non-human experience through anthropomorphism, by putting human attributes onto the insect, but bear with me as I do. It is a bit of a habit of mine. And the story of the caterfly or butterpillar is really a fascinating one when interpreted through the anthropomorphic eye. To leave it out of a book about the quiet revolutions that can take place in the face of collapse would literally be a literary crime.

But I focus on the insatiable appetite of the caterpillar primarily because it bears striking similarity, in some ways, to the long stretches we go through in life where we get eaten alive by our own insecurities. And that in itself can make our lives feel incredibly messy. I imagine the inner critic to have an appetite like the caterpillar: absolutely formidable and seemingly unstoppable until there is nothing left to consume.

However, there are particles in the caterpillar that solely belong to the butterfly, and exclusively to the second wind of the insect's life. They are the only cells and sparks of life, called 'imaginal discs', that survive the destruction of the caterpillar and in effect are released from storage to draw together and create a very different form. The imaginal discs are essentially the seeds of the butterfly already in the caterpillar, developed while in the egg, in the prelude to even becoming the caterpillar. They are the only thing left over in the mush of the caterpillar's worst fear come upon it. And it is the protein left over in the mush from all the caterpillar's feeding days that charges up these discs to grow. The discs are there in the very beginning of conception, to be stored away until the very end, at the height of the caterpillar's demise. And they create the most miraculous new beginning in the world of all nature's miracles, through the leftovers of devastation. This is one of nature's best examples of the interconnectivity of all things.

Using all these fascinating, yet overlooked details of the caterpillar as a metaphor, it really is a beautiful thought to imagine, after hitting rock bottom, that *whatever* is left behind in the process of destruction is actually *all you need* to find your wings and soar through the next chapter of your life. Imagine you are feeling like you have come to the end of yourself, in the grip of adversity, with your worst fear upon you. You are at the edge of the cliff. Darkness is dictating and yet, actually, whatever is left of you, in the goo of emotional wreckage and/or practical ruin, is all you need in order to be reborn into the untouched and soaring essence of who you are, far beyond the reach of anything that has eaten you up until now — whether it be childhood trauma, depression, constant anxiety-ridden choices and projections, debilitating insecurities, self-hatred and other mental health issues. What if, whatever you have left over of yourself from feeling eaten alive by whatever it is that you struggle with, is all you essentially are, and all you need in order to create a second wind for yourself? A life that is more authentic than anything you have experienced up to now . . . Take a moment to just consider that. It truly is a beautiful thought.

∽

After any dealing with life's messiness, whatever you have left in your hands is all you ever need to move forward.

∽

WHEN YOUR WORST FEAR COMES UPON YOU

Sometimes, we actually need our worst fear to come upon us because the fear of it is the prison, not the outcome itself. It's the fear that obstructs our view of life and all the possibilities surrounding the outcome. It's the fear that distorts and burdens our experience of ourselves, making us feel less able than we are. It's the fear that paralyses us, freezing us in an invisible, secret nightmare of suffocating weakness and incapacitating self-doubt; a landscape of repetition, where we are victim to our frightful and anxiety-ridden imaginings spinning in our minds with no pause and no escape. It's the fear that has us dodging potentially transformative opportunities. Your worst fear may come upon you as you make your way through your adventure, but that's OK. Because this is the way to shed the fear to an extent that it no longer paralyses you. Part Two's toolkit can assist you at this particular point in your passage. Assuring yourself that everything is going to be OK, taking moments to pause and slow down, and remembering that your adventure is more than any point of struggle you are caught up in right now are always good go-tos to start off with. Acknowledging how you have come back after similar or worst challenges is also significantly encouraging.

Humans survive the harshest of realities. Look back on your life and remember what you have survived. Look back on others' lives and notice what they have survived. The expanses of the human story are simply astonishing. Broadly speaking, the ratio of survival is 100 to 1. We will survive 99 bad things before we don't, and sometimes it might be even more than that. The odds are in our favour because of our biological make-up, because of the basic instincts that drive us. Survival is rarely the issue. It's the *fear* of not surviving that corrodes and begins a spiral of decay and toxicity against our hope and sense of self. Once the fear is gone, once we are just faced with the very outcome of what we have spent all our time and energy trying to avoid, our vision is cleansed, our senses are cleared. And more often than not, we get to work, because with all that's left over, we can simply see more clearly and therefore respond with purpose, much like the imaginal discs of the caterpillar while in the chrysalis. Yes, you guessed it, the imaginal discs of the insect are intrinsically responsive, organised and focused. As soon as they are awakened, they team up and get to work creating what eventually becomes the butterfly. This is a wonderful metaphor for human transformation through hard times.

Whatever we imagined in fear, that had us gripped in a sense of powerlessness, often happens very differently from how we imagined it. The key detail is that we are left remaining after the outcome, in a surprising way. We are not wiped away. We are not destroyed like we always feared. That element of surprise is the factor to open our minds and hearts and propel us forward to the challenges of survival we face and potentially evolve through them. Can you imagine the joy and surprise of the former caterpillar when it realises there is food once again to enjoy – and the sweetest kind of food at that!

Our worst fears reveal the limits of what we know and experience of ourselves in this moment. They also unveil what we don't know, and what we are yet to experience of ourselves, just like the caterpillar. They also indicate that there is still a wonderful upgrade awaiting us, on the other side of meeting our fears, where we will form the beautiful wings that have always been a part of us. Your worst fear consumes just one aspect of your spectrum of thought and feeling; it's actually a smaller part of you than it will often feel. When your worst fear comes upon you, that's the shell that encloses your boundless awareness of yourself cracking, so that you can experience more and explore your ever-evolving potential. Rather than simply breaking, or collapsing, or being permanently turned to mush, you are breaking open, you are breaking free. It just often feels scary and painful at the beginning because we assume and identify that our caterpillar life up to now is all there is for us. But the mush, the collapse, the shattering is all just a part of fuelling up the wonderful and buried phenomenon that makes you, you.

So, on your adventure, do not feel perpetually disheartened if and when your worst fear comes knocking at your door, and your prospects and valuable aspects of your life and journey suddenly turn to 'goo'. Remind yourself in the disappointment of the story and cycle of the caterfly and keep your eyes alert and heart open to the hidden possibilities in such an occurrence. It could be the mushy beginnings of your most incredible comeback and regeneration to date. The goo is often a goo(d) sign, accompanied by lots of promise.

Write it out

1. Recount an experience in your past where you realised the fear of the outcome was worse than the outcome itself and what that showed you.

2. Do you have any 'mushy', 'gooey' areas in your life, right now? Areas where you might feel a sense of devastation, displacement or threatening change? How can you reframe this portion of your life with the reference points of the caterfly cycle? Is it possible through any of the current details to relate them to the factors needed for a new beginning or a rising of some kind? Try to draw links in these areas to the different stages of the metamorphosis. The caterpillar (lava) stage, the transition (pupa) stage and the butterfly (adult) stage.

3. Put your storyteller hat on and write the story of the butterfly, as you see it. Feel free to use anthropomorphism and write about yourself like the butterfly is you. Here's an example:

> *She thought the darkness was coming for her, but really it was coming to set her free. She thought it was coming to suffocate her, but it wanted to enclose her in its mystery and give life to the quietest, deepest dreams she carried. Sometimes it's the darkest hours that fuse the brightest glimmers inside us to finally be seen, to finally stand out, so we can be guided by them. She thought her life was over.*
>
> *But really it was just beginning.*
>
> *She thought she would crawl through life forever, picking up whatever was around her, carrying on her shoulders whatever was put on her, unable to stop herself from absorbing the good, the bad and the ugly, whatever she was*

exposed to. She didn't realise she had wings growing inside her from the start. She didn't realise she was on the right road towards a life of autonomy.

It was hard to believe the darkness was a friend, a guide, a companion set to bring the best out of her, set to rid her of all that held her back. It was hard to let go, to trust. Just at the point when she felt everything had collapsed inside her, she had nothing to hold on to, that's when the darkness told her to resist all the more, to hold on, to push through the collapsing as hard as she could.

She didn't understand. She didn't know what the darkness wanted. As she resisted, the darkness encouraged her to soften. When she softened, then the darkness told her to resist.

It seemed a cruel game. One she wanted to get out of and so she started to tear through the darkness. She fought and resisted until she broke through and was hit by the light. And when she came back to life and slowly stood on her legs, she looked back and saw wings strong and wide. The dark shell was left behind.

She couldn't believe how small the cocoon actually was. It had consumed her sky and her soil for what felt like so long. But, in fact, she could now carry the cocoon on her wings if she wanted. Yes, she could carry the darkness. And that's when the darkness said, 'I made you strong on the outside. And I made you soft on the inside. I have done what I was meant to do.'

And that was the last push she needed. She knew she could fly anywhere now. There was nothing she had to be wary of. Because both the light and darkness took turns to look after her, depending on whatever it was she needed.

CHAPTER SIXTEEN

Listen Out for the Songs Along the Mountains

Not too many years ago, it dawned on me that I needed to take a sudden brave turn in my own life. Life couldn't have been any brighter at the time. I had worked hard on myself for many months, to be gently enraptured in the openings of my mind and heart over that period. I had come through the darkest years and months of my life, induced by my first late miscarriage. I had just given birth to my third daughter at home a handful of months previously, in what could only be called a thrilling and empowering labour. (My other experiences of labour had been completely the opposite!) I was breastfeeding without the extortionate pain and tears of my experiences before. These were huge milestones for me in the recent tumultuous landscapes of my voyage through motherhood. I looked back on my life and there was a golden thread sewn through all the significant moments, tragic and beautiful, making sense out of my passage so far in ways that meant I could only trust life more. And I wanted to. I was excited to see where this was all going. I felt like I was winning. I was running way ahead of my fears, my past sorrows and any enduring self-doubt. And then, one day, out of nowhere, an unexpected bill came into my life and knocked me off this top-of-the-world moment I had been enjoying, in one clean strike. I landed on the ground below the mountains and the clouds, with a hard thud. All the strength I had felt, the warrior powers, the connectedness, the lightness and the soft love suddenly became deactivated in my senses, and I felt I was immediately sinking.

Out of nowhere, the dam had broken, and I was engulfed in this flurry of strong, negative emotion. My fingers were trembling. We couldn't pay the bill. I wasn't working. I was self-employed. And I was on maternity leave. We had just about enough money to get us by, but nothing extra. It was one of my worst fears come upon me. To be vulnerable, to be dependent and to not have enough to provide for my children. My fear dragged me irrationally through a number of worst-case scenarios, all in the space of a couple of minutes. There my imagination was working against me. The sudden shift in my feelings was unrestrained and I felt sweepingly weak and gripped in intimidation.

I couldn't believe how a letter could have me give up everything that meant so much to me in my consciousness of sense and emotion, within a moment or two. It was such a sudden descent in feeling that it woke me up. It dawned on me with such clarity that my fundamental ideas of myself were still largely based on (mistaken) unconscious assumptions about my supposed innate deficiency. Here was a mountain suddenly in my way (the said bill), and it was showing me that these beautiful feelings and truths I had been gently dancing with over the last few weeks took up only surface ground in my life. But I needed them to go deeper. I needed them to become my roots. I realised, through this, that my waking life was still based on me essentially feeling like I was not enough. I had just tried to grow good things on top of it. Even in my moment of glory, right in the middle of my lap of honour, I couldn't hold my joy, my growing sense of strength and pride in who I was becoming, at this new sighting of the Great Mess. Feelings of inferiority, insecurity and self-doubt went a lot deeper. And this was nothing to be ashamed of. But it was everything to change.

I felt righteously frustrated by my automatic responses. I felt protective over this recent time and how conscientious I had been with my healing and self-care. And how I really felt I deserved this time of feel-good. It was like daylight robbery, happening right in front of me, happening right inside of me! And I declared enough was enough. I was tired of being riddled with these painful feelings for at least two of the near four decades I had been alive. Even now in this season of new beginnings, these old feelings could snatch all the new away, in a single moment. I had to change something. I had to change my approach. I was done with feeling so small in the face of challenges that demanded more of me than I even believed in. I got to work and with unflinching focus (probably from the strength I had demonstrated and grown over the past few months). I started coaching myself out of this automatic response mechanism. I essentially put my paralysing fears in a straitjacket. Every time my inner critic would rise to tear me apart, I quickly rebutted it with affirmations and fortified truths about my character. I went to work over all the goodness, bravery and muscle I had shown over the last months and years gone by. I went on the offensive by growing my sense of worthiness and homing in on talking to myself and about myself in a positive way. It was also time to reconceptualise my story so that these important details would be automatically highlighted from now on.

I gave the bill some context in the wider canvas of adulting. I placed it in the broader landscape of life over the past few years, which made all that I initially damned as lack turn into examples of growth, right in front of my very eyes. I reminded myself of how many other people struggle too; that a lot of people find paying their bills difficult and sometimes impossible. That despite not being able to be in a place of financial stability for my family in the way I had always wanted to be, my children knew nothing of it so far. We always had enough money for them to not know we needed more. I reminded myself that what I lacked in my bank account, I made up for in my heart, my integrity, my bravery, my consciousness. And I addressed my guilt. That was the real turning point.

I challenged the guilt I felt, thoughtfully and reasonably. I questioned why I shouldn't be able to struggle; why my struggle had to be an indication that I was failing in my life. Could it not be a sign that I was trying with all my might, each and every month, to live out what I had found to be true? Did it not show my bravery to keep going, to face a force seemingly too large for me to subdue month in and month out, and yet I persisted? My vision and sense of being was going through a quiet transformation. These were the truths missing in my perspective up to now. My shoulders relaxed even more, my hands unclenched and my stomach unknotted itself. Nothing had changed on the outside, but from the inside, I was once again walking through a new door.

I started to reframe my story from a place of gain and possibility, rather than deficit and imagined loss. Every time my imagination would play games on me, I would focus in on the present moment and get back to chopping wood and carrying water.[1] I declared the mountains ahead of me would become my friends (this might offer insight into how I carved out this concept of the Great Mess being a gentle giant). With all the moments of self-doubt that came my way, I kept repeating to myself that the mountains in my life showed up to help transport me to some beautiful sights, scenery and views that I would never find without them. The mountains wanted me to get to the top. I mean, this bill obviously wanted us to find a way to pay it! I kept reciting, in all the ways I could, that I was able, that I had something to offer this world, that this mountain in my life was partly here to prove it, that I would find my way. There was nothing beneficial in feeling like life was against me, that these mountains had shown up specifically to trip me up. I decided to turn these ideas about life that had haunted me all through my adult years right around. The mountains weren't against me. They were rooting for me. It effectively turned my inner world around too. I haven't looked back since.

∿

Mountains don't show up to trip you up.

∿

A REFRAMING VISUALISATION

Let's try something now. As we are coming up to our final moments together, here is a visual meditation that is intended to inspire you to keep an eye out for the mountains along your way that are rooting for you too, so that you can listen out for their songs as you walk. It's another reconceptualisation to add to your growing library and I use the 'What if' perspective (see page 143) here too. Put it in your backpack for when you feel you need to reframe your circumstances:

Take a moment to imagine a life for yourself where you don't have to look over your shoulder. Where you don't have to check behind you all the time. Imagine a life where you don't feel alone because nothing in life can truly isolate you. What if the mountains you have climbed were not out to get to you, or into your head, or slow you down, or tire you out, or defeat you?

What if the mountains you have contended with were giants who lowered themselves to the ground so that you could climb on their backs and then find the most beautiful, breathtaking scenery and views of life? And they did it because they knew it would have your hope and your energy renewed and reborn all in one? What if there was no enemy? What if there was nothing to defeat? Only the full spectrum of life to integrate, including sadness, loss, failure and, of course, messiness?

Imagine how easy dancing might be if there was no need to wear armour, because nothing was out to attack you. Imagine if life was just full of unintentional accidents, the kind that happen when there's lots happening and nothing is slowing down. And, over time, we just get better skilled at navigating through it.

What if every mountain you have climbed to the top of and down again, in this promising life of yours, cheers for you today? Knowing that with any other mountain that comes your way, you will find great heights within you and be drawn to notice the most beautiful sights around you and beneath you.

What if the mountain knows that the only way you will ever believe you are giant is if you see what a giant might see and hear what a giant might hear? And that's why it is stationed where it is, or at least that is one of the reasons. Because the mountain knows it is the closest thing to a giant in this world.

What if the mountain can see your capacity better than you can see it right now? And the only way to prove to you the scale of your strength is to demand it?

There are a lot of questions here for you to delve into and I am not saying this is an entirely accurate or balanced perspective. But it is another way to approach life. And you can utilise aspects of it to help balance out your own. It offers fresh insight, available as inspiration to open your heart and mind to new possibilities. It actually works as a steady foundation to mature and develop. It challenges our own uninvestigated ideas that emerge in defiance and takes away the sting of feeling like the harsh things that happen are personal. You don't necessarily have to make a home in this perception, but at least see what you can take from it.

With these ideas as genuine interpretations to absorb into your own vision, you can learn to walk boldly into the day with the chorus of mountains behind you. All of them that you have danced on the top of. All of them that have made you breathe heavily. They sing of how giant you, yourself, are. They sing of how strong and able you are. They sing of your unbreakable spirit. This complements the positive gains mindset we explored in Chapter Thirteen (see page 181).

I can imagine you came to this book feeling weary. But maybe that's also partly because you have thought you are smaller than you are. And you approach the moments of life coming your way, whether they are sprinkled with challenge or bliss, like you are not big enough to hold them. The mountains can guide you to heights that suit you and the ingredients you need for the dreams you have. You just have to take the challenge to climb them.

Mountains and new beginnings go together in my mind. You climb a mountain and you find a view of the world you have never seen before. Something is born inside you. Something new. And then it begins to form, in your soul, your ribcage, your beautiful mind. Surrender to the path of the mountain and let the songs of mountains behind you carry you as you do. They sing about you. They sing about the new beginning up ahead – that if you just keep on putting one foot in front of the other, not even your worst fears can get in the way. Yes, not even all those fears that have held you prisoner up to now. Sure, you might have to climb a mountain to get to it, but you've done it before. And you can do it again. That's why the mountains sing for you. They want to point you to certain extraordinary sights that will make you feel reborn.

Write it out

1. Write about a huge mountain you are facing at the moment or have recently climbed over. Consider anything positive it can or has offered you. Imagine the experience with it from a point of feeling supported by everything you have achieved in the past.

2. Imagine the feeling of getting to the top of it and write about the experience using your five senses to develop the imagining.

3. What stands in your way? What supports you on your way? Write down a couple of ways you can focus more on what supports you and put them into your backpack. What habits will they replace?

CHAPTER SEVENTEEN

Look Out for the Younger You

I have already mentioned that we leave pieces of who we are on the trail of our self-discovery and expression, all the way through life. Some pieces we leave out of choice. The decision is an intentional and empowering one. Whether it be a few sacred moments of transcendental, dreamy thought or echoes of bellowed laughter from nights enjoyed with friends and loved ones, to steamy early mornings of heart-racing romance or a gesture of love we showed someone in daring to reveal our naked hearts. We are active participants in these uplifting moments and sometimes initiators of these gifts of exchange that become figurative mementoes in our journey.

This aspect of our experience on this planet can be deeply comforting and bittersweet. It's why we like revisiting places we have enjoyed special moments in. It's why we have literal happy places or favourite ways to get home. Every time we return, on a visceral level, we experience a mysterious sense of reunion. We find again those pieces of ourselves we left there, in those simple and significant connections. This is why we will say to ourselves, 'I feel more me when I am here' or 'I feel so at peace.'

It's a piece of magic in this world, a chemistry of wizardry that we don't pay enough attention to. It's an effective way to catch your breath and gather perspective, away from intense circumstances that are heavy and taxing to wade through. The kind of moments where you are just pushing and pushing and pushing and nothings feels like it's going to give. You are exhausted from the constant labour, wondering to yourself if life is actually just about climbing and struggling. It's really important when travelling through this kind of terrain along your adventure that you find spaces where you can see the world around you, outside of that intensity. Because life is more than the pushing and the constant struggle. It's also about catching a fire-red sunset in the glowing sky. It's about poetry that breaks your heart and music that mends your heart immediately after. We need to steal moments away from the storms that come. That's why our eyes are designed to note the rainbow immediately after.

These moments of reunion are often so physical, using our senses as the bridge for communication. They are the kind of memories you can smell coming, those seconds where you are transported from your present moment into the eternal recall of that very episode you are remembering. Time is blurred. The past and present become remarkably inseparable. We sit deeper in ourselves. There is nowhere to get to right now, because it is all here. These simple moments of remembering and reunion are deeply spiritual in the most natural of ways. It might be certain smells you come across or songs on the radio you haven't heard in years that transport you. But the point is, in your first moments of such a melody or scent, you left a piece of yourself with it, so each time you smell or hear that delight again, you might feel yourself in a renewed way.

These tangible moments that reaffirm our human experience are significant . . . down to the tastes of certain foods that remind you of being at your grandmother's table while she told you her stories. Or the sound of certain birds singing that take you back to exhales of freedom in your youth as you used to walk along the river, canal, brook or lake. We need to nourish our hearts by reuniting with these kinds of moments again and again. They give meaning to what other-wise can be a mechanical and monotonous existence. They soften the experience when the seas of life get rough. Treasure them. Carry them. They are as much a part of your life (if not more) than any expression of the Great Mess is.

~

Use the shatterings brought about by the Great
Mess to go looking for those pieces even more.

~

I imagine this to be a fun and playful dimension in the unravelling of our eternal stories. It is intimate and encouraging. There are pieces of ourselves everywhere: in different people we meet and don't meet; in stories we hear and may never hear; in experiences we have and may never have. But like tiny pieces of a mosaic, we are scattered (in a beautiful and fascinating way) and so we seek ourselves out every day. It's what makes the adventure of living both challenging and meaningful. To come back home at the end of each day with a little more expressed of our hearts and a little more reclaimed of our souls is very reassuring, and is enough to make anyone feel contented and happy to be alive.

PICKING UP THE PIECES

But, as I have mentioned before, there are aspects of ourselves that we lose touch with without really recognising it or acknowledging the loss as it happens. Through tragedy and trauma, events that we don't really have any control over, we function through the paralysing and debilitating strain of shock. In survival mode we let go of much of our sense of self. It's a strategy of survival that has got us through the many collisions of past heartbreaks, but it also leaves us feeling untrusting of ourselves and life. Because we are fragmented. Aspects of who we are, are seemingly estranged. And so, we feel less and less ourselves. And our hearts shut down in accordance. We continue to leave pieces of ourselves behind with each collision and, in our desperate focus to survive, to, in effect, get out of the ditch, we forget to pick up those pieces. We just move on. We forget to recover, and the work that takes. Often it seems we don't have time for it. And then we get to a time in our lives when we look at ourselves in the mirror and we can't recognise the person who looks back at us.

We have come full circle. Take a look back at the poem right at the start of this book. There have been so many readings of it and it has been shared so many times that I know it will mean a thousand different things to different people. And that's beautiful. But it means a lot to me on a personal level and I can share more about it now that we have got to this point together. I wrote it during the time when I began my own internal trail, my own adventure to stop running away and start walking forward and looking out for those pieces I had lost along the way as I did. Pieces I hadn't realised I was letting go of at the time. Pieces that I had wanted to actually keep. And this is when I realised the role of the two different trails, and the differences in reuniting with pieces of ourselves we willingly give away and pieces that have been snatched from us.

I first got a glimpse of that girl again, as I committed to getting to the bottom of my thoughts and feelings I had buried inside; all the things I pretended not to feel and not to think. This was a rigorous enterprise which entailed:

- Admitting my deepest and most secret feelings as I became aware of them, rather than habitually stuffing them back inside when they showed up.
- Journaling and writing out conversations with myself and other people that I wanted closure and understanding from.
- Watching my thoughts before welding them into my perspective.
- Becoming aware of my behaviour from a more objective point of view.
- Acknowledging my mistakes and not trying to explain them, but just sitting in the remorse.
- Appreciating that if my life seemed broken, it was because I was broken. It was because I had a broken heart. But to really meet my heart, I also needed to get real about what having a broken heart had created for me – like distorted (broken) ideas of myself, my relationships and my contribution to them, and of course my relationship with life.

This was a time of deep unravelling. But every now and again, in emptying myself, I discovered some precious finds. I became more compassionate and approachable. I was more vulnerable. And because of that I could experience my life so much more. The walls between me and life were decreasing, my vision was clearing and life in all its simplicity and ordinariness felt more like my home. I felt safer because I wasn't feeding into this idea that I had to remain hidden. Yes, getting more honest had me feeling safer in myself, because, apart from all the dark feelings that came up, I also couldn't deny that I knew a lot more than I often made out. This awareness was surprisingly empowering. I had dumbed myself down in wearing masks and pretending to myself. And now I wasn't doing that. My back was straightening.

∽

There is a profound sense of joy and resilience that
rushes through your bones when you decide there
is more for you than hiding or running away.

∽

As the walls were decreasing between life and me, I was also able to get closer to the girl I used to be and, in the passage to meet her, life became more electric. I could feel the kiss of the sun on my skin. I felt the warmth of the air breathe new life into me. When something made me laugh, I laughed wholeheartedly. As I made my way through the labyrinth of my past to get back my pieces, I saw her. And she was vulnerable. Her soul was naked. Her yes meant yes and her no meant no. She didn't know that masks existed. She didn't have any walls that boxed her in. She was out in the fields. No wonder she had sunflowers for eyes and fireworks still bursting in her soul. She was riding along the essence of life, in all its beauty, in all its ugliness, in all its order and chaos too. But it all balanced itself out.

It was when the balance tipped over and life became a lot uglier than it was beautiful, that's when I first started losing my pieces. That's when we all start to lose sight of that essence. And naturally so; it's instinctive and protective. That's why we always need to hold on to the beautiful aspects of life. It's also how we protect our hearts from becoming resentful. When the ugly outweighs the beauty, that's when we tend to hide away our vulnerability.

WHEN VULNERABILITY GETS UNCOMFORTABLE

This was a colossal insight for me and I spent months unpacking it. I had to revisit the ugly chapters in my story to better own the narratives I had lived by and make peace with them. But the pieces that were taken from me, through events that were entirely out of my control as a little girl, or as a teenager, or even as a young adult, were snatched or lost in the 'messiest' of times. And through all my deepening honesty, the epiphanies that came and the lucid and attentive wandering, I saw a recurring pattern.

In all those times, I had needed someone to help me deal with the particular 'mess', but that person (who sometimes would change from event to event), for whatever reason, never showed up in a way that met my legitimate needs. It hurt to admit it. It hurt to allow myself to be that vulnerable and confess my needs like that. But that girl inside me needed me to come through for her now. So I did my best to not turn away from any pain.

The poem conveys the need for the younger you to feel safe. Safe enough to come out again. In order to 'call them back again' and bring all the pieces of who you are, essentially under the same roof, they therefore need you to be the person you needed around when you were younger. They need to know that, when the mess comes again (because life will always be messy), it will be dealt with in the best possible way, or at least that enough effort will be made to do that. Because that's what didn't happen in the past and that was the reason why they had to go into hiding. This is when taking responsibility for your life and the younger you becomes the next crucial stage in your healing and rebirth.

Rising up

Take a moment now to briefly think on some of the uglier times in your upbringing or your past and how it might have turned out differently if your genuine and appropriate needs had been met at the time. Regardless of the 'mess' that happened, think about how it was dealt with and then consider how it could have been handled. Imagine feeling comfortable and safe enough to talk through all the complicated feelings that arose through such disarray. Imagine *not* being shouted at, because outbursts were controlled. Imagine *not* being ignored as your world was crumbling. Imagine *not* feeling on your own because the others involved didn't run away at the sight of the hard reality needing to be met. Imagine any abuse and manipulation *stopping* because of immediate remorse and regret. Imagine being comforted, reassured, considered and supported by those who were in the official position to do that. Imagine your heart being seen and your feelings being heard. Imagine heads *not* diving into the sands at the sight of calamity or of your initial reactions. Imagine those people in your life being held accountable, by other level-headed people around them. Furthermore, imagine them holding themselves accountable. Because had you had that, there's a high chance you might have found the pieces lost in the upheaval soon enough after. Perhaps your wounds and all the damage wouldn't have gone so deep. And perhaps you wouldn't even need to call the younger you back in the first place.

Your younger self needs to know that they've got someone who will do their part to facilitate what you have just imagined in the paragraph above. That they have access to a person who develops the kind of character to respond to difficult moments and not run, hide or pretend away what's really going on. Because you have started making better choices and you have grasped opportunities to face yourself, to mature and grow, and shed bad habits that would put them in unnecessary danger. This is the beautiful opportunity we get to grasp when difficult moments arise. We get to break cycles and generational chains that made us victims of harsh and horrible experiences in our adult past and when we were younger by working hard to be the person we needed in those times:

- To not turn away at the sight of complexity.
- To stay around and clean up the mess.
- To stay in the hard conversations.
- To not give up.
- To not take stress out on others.
- To hold back from over-criticising yourself.
- To change the angle and lens you are looking through so you can take more information in.
- To not shun the parts of yourself that need the most love and attention.
- To not belittle others who think and see differently.
- To be teachable.
- To say I love you.
- To say I'm sorry.
- To allow regret and remorse to cleanse your vision.
- To be vulnerable.
- To ask when you need help.
- To admit when you don't know what to do.
- To make better choices.
- To hold yourself accountable.
- To not allow your wounds to hold you in the corner as prisoner anymore.
- To not run away.

In the face of harsh moments, whatever wasn't done for you that should have been, made life immediately uglier, more hazardous and complicated for you. And the younger you is now worth your commitment to grow these responses in yourself.

You can become this character in your story yourself. This is how you become your own hero. And yes, you guessed it, the learning ground for these attributes to develop is in the face of chaos. It's in similar situations where you didn't get what you needed when you were younger. You need to look out for what you remember of the younger you from now. You need to re-parent them through the gift of reassurance (see page 121) and talk to them with kindness (see page 138). In doing so, you will reunite and swiftly become a force to be reckoned with, that no manifestation of the Great Mess will be able to subdue. This is how you get the most out of your adventure. Nothing is more powerful in this world than personal unification and the healing process that makes that possible.

Dealing with the Great Mess is not separate to your healing. It's another one of life's marvels that puts so much right in our lives. It's true that the issues we've carried from our childhood and certain experiences we go through in our adulthood often lie at the feet of others. But because we are essentially the most powerful of participants in the crafting of our own ongoing story, when we take this position, it creates prevailing ripples, for our own personal sense of selfhood and for those we love too. Whatever drove our younger selves into hiding is not our fault. Please, always remember that. But we can now make it safe for them to come out again, and the joy and vigour we can have together is irreplaceable.

That poem was the result of committing to become the person I needed when I was younger, despite how challenging that might be, despite the implications and the layers, and what I had to face, give up and let go of. But this was how I got her attention again and slowly built a new bridge of trust towards her that she might cross. So that she could feel the sun on her brow again. So that *I* could feel the sun on my brow again. If I hadn't done that, it wouldn't have mattered what music I played. *This* was the effort. *This* was the kindness I always needed. And now I just want to make little me proud. We all deserve that.

Write it out

1. List some of the pieces you have given away freely of yourself and write a little about them. (Think of moments, activities, places and people that make you feel more yourself.) What is the feeling you get when you reunite with them? When was the last time?

2. Think back again to a time when someone close to you really let you down. And you could never tell them how you felt. Think back to how much you needed that person to hear the truth. But imagine if they had been willing to hear you. What would you say to them if you could?

3. Write a letter to your younger you. The person who could wear their heart on their sleeve because they had no need to hide. That wild, powerful, vibrant young soul. Remember a time when you were so free and include it in the letter. Suggest some ways in which you can reconnect.

Conclusion

I have never been good at goodbyes. But you are more than ready now for your adventure – if you haven't begun it already, that is. You now know better what you are up against – that the battleground is more inside than outside. You know better how to get by and how to deal with the challenges that might come up, and you know why you are perfect for the mission. You also know what to keep an eye out for when in transit. I am also hoping that you are able to better pick up when whatever is going on around you externally is comparably marginal in importance to the story happening underneath its surface, and inside you. Always look out for what doors of perception might open up for you in your interior world. Any adventure outside is only as great as the adventure within.

You might look back on your life now, as I have done many a time, and recoil at the fact that too many days of it have been saturated in struggle of some kind and that ratio in itself has worn you down over time, leaving you automatically frightened and intimidated by adversity in general. It's a long road to get that out of your system, but frame this adventure at hand with this very prerogative. It is the passage to do exactly that: to wash your faculties of old, automatic, fearful reactions to hard times, so that, when they do arrive, you can envision and locate the possibilities and opportunities for growth they bring with them instead.

And yes, old habits die hard. But they can and do die. And there is a spectrum of intelligent responsiveness, adaptability and resolve inside you that is older than those habits, and it goes far deeper. To find it, you have to look within. To look within, you have to open your heart. Your open heart is the missing piece in all the puzzles, all the maps and all your accomplishments in this field of experience coming your way. In fact, your heart opening or staying open is the very power you need in any messy circumstance. It is the way to access your potential. It is the way to access any veiled life-giving properties in the chaotic conditions you go out to face. And if ever your heart feels solidly closed, just begin with getting honest about that, brutally honest if necessary, and slowly but surely, the locks inside will turn. We imagine the power of the Great Mess to lie in the devastation it brings, but actually, its greatest power lies in the promise of transformation that opens once we decide we will run towards the chaos, through it and beyond it.

In a similar way we can't remain existing in this world if our physical hearts are in constant shutdown, nor can we really ever comprehend our authentic power, the possibilities for our lives and the passages of love and self-discovery we want to go on if we continue to pass through our days with our hearts predominantly closed, protected and hidden away on an emotional level. Regardless of whatever you face, more than the particular (and often scary) details of it, the most important question you need to answer in word and deed is, are you willing to take a risk? The old habits that might have ensured your survival and kept you safe and insulated enough up to now, may have also left you deeply unsatisfied and maybe even a little (or a lot) resentful and suppressed too. Because it's opening your heart and keeping it open that creates all-round access to your joy and power. That's what transforms your experience, that's what will keep you going in difficult times and that's what will transform your very life. And the Great Mess, like everything else in your life, will succumb to the assignment and assist you as you make this happen for yourself – once you make it your main agenda.

∽

You have the power. You are the power.

∽

Once you start to get a grip of your perspective, approaches and choices, you realise you are the game changer in your life. You hold the power and are the emblem of power in all your circumstances. And acknowledging this fact more and more will awaken all the power inside so that you can start using it to work up some magic for you – like feeling deeper, lasting peace, a more integrated sense of self, feeling more plugged into your courage, and deepening your own journey of healing and self-actualisation.

I haven't written these words wanting to imply that any of this is easy. The work required to connect the truths and principles explored in this book and then integrate and slowly own them in your life is the antithesis to all you have grown used to over the years. But I just want to also say that you are worth all the effort and commitment it will take to do this. Your life is worth it. Your potential is worth it. The younger you is worth it. Your future joy is worth all the effort it will take to penetrate your fears as you hold them, yet do not follow them. And I am genuinely excited for you to experience this shift in your life. It will look good on you, like it was always for you to own and call yours. Your open heart, and life lived in and with your open heart, is worth any of the labour it might demand to get it open. All the blood, the sweat and any tears – let them be the channel for all your bottled-up energy to be processed and pass along, so that you can feel spaciousness inside you to create and participate in new, life-giving experiences.

I bet nearly all of us have good reason to shut down our hearts forever and live through them that way. There are countless things we shouldn't have witnessed or been put through. But with any kind of shutdown that lingers long after the aftermath of such circumstances and events, it's us who suffer in the end. Life dramatically changes as a landscape that we peer out into and engage with, and our experience of self intensely deteriorates as well. This is what my grandmother was trying to get across to me in that dream I shared with you at the beginning of the book (see page 19). I have thought so many times about what she was really trying to articulate and now, in coming to the end of our time together, I am drawn to it again.

It was like she was looking over from across the veil and saying to me:

> I know what the harsher side of life will make you do. It made me do it a hundred times over. And I did it for good reason. Nothing and no one can ever take that away from me. But . . . it was me who paid in the end. It was me who missed even more, because of what I lost. And peering now into the landscape of eternal unravelling, and with all I have before me (as spirit) and all I have (in being alive as a human) behind me, what I gave up because of how horrific the pain and loss was, just wasn't worth it. To lose something so precious to you and then to willingly give away moments of promise and beauty, because there's a possibility you

could get hurt again, only means you are losing twice. I wish I hadn't lost twice. I wish that, in all that was taken from me, I had turned around and run towards life, demanding something back, in return. Something as great, something as significant. I wish I had dared to demand back some kind of soulful recompense, shaking my fists to the skies and crying out, 'You owe me.' And then turned towards my life, to go looking for the experiences and the perspectives that would help manage the horrible losses I carried as memories in my body for the rest of my days.

The chaos and devastation in life, in all its tragedies and horrors, will have you turn away. But don't turn away for too long, darling. Open when you can. Choose intimacy. Choose new beginnings. Choose vulnerability. Choose healing. Choose surprising yourself. Yes, don't think you know everything about yourself. Be willing to get things wrong. Be willing to learn new things about you. Go against the grain that tells you to keep running, that tells you to keep hardly existing, to keep surviving, to keep hiding, to keep trembling, to keep dodging. When you have done enough crying and reviewing, go against the grain and grab the hand of life and go for more, not less, even if you limp forward. There are beautiful sights of your world you only get to see when you commit to the arduous uphill climb that will get you there. At some point, make the decision, go against the grain. Because who are we to say what is waiting for us down the path anyway?

It now makes me think that perhaps this is the unrehearsed goal of this mysterious life – to see how many times in our lives we are able to find our way back to tenderness and trust. And be willing to reach out beyond our confines, despite the bumps and kinks in the road that we assume are telling us to stay in our places. And that we do it without bypassing all the instinctive emotions that also carry their own kind of gift of release and wisdom too.

The Great Mess isn't your nemesis. It's difficult terrain to outgrow the processes and habits we automatically fall into. We have to undo the impairment and unlock the chains around our minds because of the years we have spent reactively living, and delve deeper into a plain of seeing and experiencing that is both expansive and consolidative. This begins with pulling away from shame-induced dialogue and hostility towards yourself and life, and, in turn, building up your sense of worthiness through some of the approaches in your new toolkit. Self-reassurance and self-compassion are fundamental to this. As is reconceptualisation and the freedom, daring and possible fun involved in the process of reframing your dealings with mess into unlikely adventures of self-discovery.

We put so much focus and emphasis on the mess itself, that we miss the most significant and powerful component in any circumstance – ourselves and our choices. Who we are and the position we take in dealing with any part of life; the bright, the dark and the dull; the good, the bad and the ugly. That is the storehouse of power and possibility in every moment that comes our way. We are sustained in times of difficulty by paying attention to our lives (inside and out) and not turning away, from ourselves or the challenges up ahead. Because demons do need to be silenced, and fiery dragons do need to be either slain or flown on, and your fears need to be proven wrong so that you can be liberated enough to go out in the direction of your dreams, even when they seem like a distant cloud hovering over wild seas. You have the power to do this. Remember, you *are* the power in this dynamic.

The Great Mess will bring those demons and dragons to you, alongside the fears, so that you can rise up to be the hero of your story and this very adventure and get yourself across those tumultuous seas. To put you on an even keel, you just have to give more focus to any one or more of the following:

- Getting out of the shame game (this is the biggest weapon in your backpack).
- Becoming your own cheerleader and support, and being mindful of the things you say to yourself (look for the 'maybes' in the mayhem).
- Learning how to use your perceptions to empower you through your imagination so that you can reconceptualise your struggles into adventures and missions.
- Remembering that your troubles are part of being human, rather than any irredeemable failing on your part and learning to put a sense of worth and function to your tough moments in the past.
- Processing your grief so that, soon enough, when you sense any overpowering feelings emerging, it doesn't have you shutting off and down for too long.
- Opening up the playing field by not getting so caught up in purpose and outcomes, but more in expanding your experience and relationship with life through the principles of storytelling.
- Giving yourself permission to take breaks and breaths when you need to.
- Learning to believe that you are worthy of any of the wonderful things that might result from hard times.
- Getting fixated on the empowering details of your life, rather than the disempowering ones.
- Taking up the challenge of being the person you needed when you were younger when messy circumstances occur.

And the list goes on . . . You have so many approaches and principles now that can equip you for each meeting with the Great Mess and lean on the ones that really speak to you. Follow your intuition and the words and ideas that stand out to you the most. You are not inadequate in this cause, like you have felt many times up to now. And hopefully, in taking on the suggestions in this book, you are feeling that your backpack is full of what you need to move forward.

We must learn to overlook the 'problems' the mess creates and hunt for the power it can evoke inside us. This is how you will find the sunflowers and the fireworks inside your soul, the kinds that don't die or run out, no matter what tough times come up along your path. And they wait in those places in your heart that have been around a lot longer than any fear, any trauma, any threshold of grief. So, meet these inevitable struggles for what they truly are: gateways to go through and get beyond, so that you can experience *your* essence, *your* power, *your* joy. Because that's the magical happening that makes the lows and blows suffered along the way worthwhile. Yes, *you* make it all worth it. The power that you have inside, once awoken, truly knows no bounds.

And power to the mess for unveiling that.

Do you know that day yet?
The one when you wake up and your mind feels your own
And all the voices have gone quiet
And you are not looking over your shoulder.
And you feel like you can stay in bed for as long or as little as
    you want.
Because no one is watching. No one is judging.
And you are no longer choking
And you can hear yourself breathing
Because there is a song there.
And in the song is poetry you wrote so long ago.
When you lived for waking.
When you lived for the sun birthing herself again and again.
And you put your ear right up close to your exhale
Like a shell from the sea
Because it's a sound you've longed all your adult life to hear.
Nothing is breathing you.
No one is breathing down your neck.
Your eyes, they open and you can see beyond the clearing.
The fog is behind you.
And you smell freedom on your skin.
You feel it dance within.
Because you took your power back.
You took your mind back and your life
And now you greet the day

With your vows and your confetti,

'in good times and bad'

Because life has made a beautiful song out of you.

And out of all that lasting, temporary misery.

It was always going to.

That kind of mystery written in your eyes could always sense it
    coming.

And now you are, once again, willing to give your everything.

Yes, brave, beating heart, that day is coming.[1]

Endnotes

Preface
1 Lourie, S.C., 2018. 'Be Proud of your Proof' from *Goddess:Woman, Butterfly:Human*. APS Publications (first edition), p142.

Introduction
1 Lourie, S.C., 2018. 'You Carry the Skies in your Womb' from *Goddess:Woman, Butterfly:Human*. APS Publications (first edition), p30.

Chapter Three: Making the Mess Your Teacher
1 Frankl, V., 2004. *Man's Search for Meaning*. Rider, p. 75.
2 Sones, B. and R., n.d. Strange but true: 95 per cent of brain activity is unconscious. *The Oklahoman*. Retrieved from https://eu.oklahoman.com/story/lifestyle/2018/10/09/strange-but-true-95-percent-of-brain-activity-is-unconscious/60496296007/.
3 Lourie, S.C., 2018. 'A Holy Surrender' from *Goddess:Woman, Butterfly:Human*. APS Publications (first edition), p69.

Chapter Four: Getting Out of the Shame Game
1 Blake, W., *c.*1818. *The Marriage of Heaven and Hell*. Houghton Library at Harvard University, copy G, object 13 [composition 1790].

Chapter Five: The Power in Our Perceptions
1 Frankl, V., 2004. *Man's Search for Meaning*. Rider, p. 75.

Chapter Six: Embrace Your Inner Storyteller

1 Lockrey, C., n.d. *The Power of Storytelling*. Retrieved from https://bcedaccess.com/wp-content/uploads/2020/09/Storytelling-1.pdf, p. 2.

2 Campbell, J., 2012. *The Hero with a Thousand Faces (The Collected Works of Joseph Campbell)*. New World Library.

Chapter Seven: The Power of Grief

1 Taken from the main themes of one of my journals, 'How the Light Gets Out', which loosely explores the beauty and power of vulnerability: *'You know, they say the cracks are where the light gets in but really I think the cracks are where "the light" gets out. Yeah, the beauty you don't realise you have. The strength inside you never get to see. The bravery you demonstrate by showing up every day, by trying, by not giving up . . . It's in the cracks that we see your light. And you're bright, darling. In your deepest, darkest days, you're just so bright.'*

2 Wikipedia, 23 Jan. 2023. Mizuta Masahide. Retrieved from https://en.wikipedia.org/wiki/Mizuta_Masahide.

Chapter Ten: Positive Self-Talk: Why 'Maybe' is a Magical Word

1 Jesse Owens Memorial Park, 2023. Links & facts. Retrieved from http://jesseowensmemorialpark.com/wordpress1/links-facts.

2 Petrocchi, N., Dentale, F. and Gilbert, P., 2019. Self-reassurance, not self-esteem, serves as a buffer between self-criticism and depressive symptoms. *Psychology and Psychotherapy: Theory, Research and Practice*, *92*(3), pp. 394–406.

Chapter Twelve: Through the Eyes of a Child

1 Gottschall, J., 2013. *The Storytelling Animal*. Mariner Books, pp. 57–8.

2 Ibid., pp. 52–53.

Chapter Thirteen: Acknowledge Your Strength and Value

1 This point is made based on David Foster Wallace's 2005 much-loved commencement speech to the graduating class at Kenyon College, that was turned into a thin book titled *This is Water: Some Thoughts, Delivered on a Significant Occasion, about Living a Compassionate Life* (Little, Brown US, 2009). Lourie, S.C., 2018. 'The Passage of *Goddess' from Goddess:Woman, Butterfly:Human*. APS Publications (first edition), p21.

2 Lourie, S.C., 2018. 'The Passage of *Goddess' from Goddess:Woman*, Butterfly:Human. APS Publications (first edition), p21.

Chapter Fourteen: Listen In for the Stories

1 Turner, M., 1996. *The Literary Mind*. Oxford University Press, p. 4.
2 Arendt, H., 1968. *Men in Dark Times*. Harcourt Brace Jovanovich.

Chapter Sixteen: Listen Out for the Songs Along the Mountains

This sentence directly borrows from a Zen proverb: 'Before Enlightenment, chop wood, carry water. After Enlightenment, chop wood, carry water.' Including it here implies keeping focus on the task at hand, despite moments of enlightening clarity along the way or wavering self-belief with the task at hand also. It also implies the capacity of the present moment, with whatever menial task we are doing, to help us not get distracted with temporary strong emotions passing through.

Conclusion

1 Lourie, S.C., 2018. 'Sweet Victory' from *Goddess:Woman, Butterfly:Human*. APS Publications (first edition), p80.

Acknowledgements

You know the saying, 'It takes a village to raise a child'? Well, I have learnt that it also takes a village to write a really solid and thought-provoking book. Moving on from trying my hand at writing novels up until around 2013, I have worked ever since in the corner of my living room, occasionally switching from my desk to the dinner table (so I can get a better view of my garden), to get my thoughts and reflections out to a growing and loving readership. I have been solely processing my own mind and digging deep into my own heart all through this time and this was the first project I have invested in that offered the dynamic of getting out of my own mind and heart to look at my words from other angles and bring out the potential power and inspiration in them even more. The passage of moving away from exclusively typing out my own unedited words from that corner in my living room to mingling with the brilliant minds and hearts of others that so believe in my work, has been quietly thrilling, nerve-racking and feverish at times, and deeply illuminating. It has allowed me to dance in between the spaces and offered a clarity that I hope will only continue. It's also offered me a growth spurt in the general craft of writing that I am so appreciative of.

There are quite a few wonderful people to thank and this list goes in no particular order (except that I do save the best until last):

To my readers across my social media platforms, who have supported me through the years and taken the walls down around their minds and hearts to allow some of my words to get in, I am indebted to you for joining me on this ride and for so long. Love to all my Resetters who have become friends. And a big shout out to all my Etsy customers who pre-ordered this book (that has ended up taking nearly five years to complete) right at the very beginning of its conception. We finally got here!

A special thanks to the Yellow Kite team and namely Carolyn for being so passionate about working together and then being so patient with me throughout. The process of getting these ideas to a publish-worthy level was indeed messy to say the least. And your capacity to adapt, extend and recalibrate the path to get here has been so wonderfully supportive. Your belief in the project has been a guiding light.

Sending much love and thanks to my editor, dear Julia, the esteemed 'book doctor' who has been a wonderful tag team partner in the final stages of the writing. What a gem you have been. Nearing that finish line when my energy was dwindling, your insights, eagerness and vision lifted me up.

And to my lovely agent, Jane, who has the uncanny habit of turning up at the right time, all I can say is wow to you and your efforts to get my work seen through all the preparation we did together. Thank you from the bottom of my heart for being so open and willing to see something in me that I couldn't quite see at the time.

Thank you to all the contributors that gave permission for me to reference them and highlight some of their words in this discourse.

To my mum and dad, thank you for all you've done for me. I

might never know the extent of it, but as I get older, I sense more and more all the effort and love you've given me, to help me on my way. To my siblings, my nieces and nephews, and my in-law family, this is one for all of us. We keep making it out of the messes of life, each and every time. I am grateful and proud of you all. To Ronald, my late stepdad, who passed away as I wrote this book, I still don't quite know what to say. It's still too raw. I just really miss you being in the world. And to my Baba, after re-reading this book a couple months after writing everything out for the last time, it is so clear for me to see how much your brave life and legacy still continues to inspire me. For all you did and for all you couldn't do, I get you and love you. Thank you for being all that you were. It was always enough and still continues to be. And to this day, I still miss your soft cheeks.

To my friends, and you know who you are, thank you for being in my life. And big love to Julliet, Jo, Hanna, and in particular, Alvin and Rachael. So, so grateful and proud of the lovely people you are. A totally warranted thank you to Tom for always greeting my projects over the years with a steadfast smile and unparalleled assistance. What a great friend you have been! To Helen, for appreciating the storyteller dying in me to always get out. I miss our walks. And special love to Annalise, who just gets it. Your wicked sense of humour gives it away. We should have been having coffee together eight years ago! But the months we had together made me feel like we have known each other for lifetimes. You were the fresh air I needed while getting this book done. Power to the Mess, my darling! (And to the podcasts! Or not? :D)

To Nova, for teaching me first that sometimes there's a lot more to your life than getting what you want, that the pain is worth it if you allow it to crack you open again and that the rebirth makes the shattering before it worthwhile. I am so grateful to have you on the other side, looking out for us all. You taught me how to fly again.

To my Sofiyah, Amelie and Kika, my source of inspiration, growth and joy, you are the bona fide reason why I stepped out to make friends with the Great Mess and heal in the first place. Your hearts keep my world spinning and I adore and feed off your pure expressions. There is nothing that makes me prouder than to be your Mama. Nothing else keeps me more on my toes as well! Yes, you read that right. Thank you for all the cuddles, the kisses, the fresh eyes and all the love. Remember, the corners are not for you. And the heights you can reach are unlimited, if you put the time in.

And finally, to Chris, the love of my life, my partner in crime and companion through the Great Mess time and time again, who showed me through word and deed that there was more for me in this life than always being on the run from myself. Thank you from the deepest and brightest in me, for e-v-e-r-y-t-h-i-n-g! And specifically, for reading through all these pages time and time again, letting me talk through all my thoughts late into the night when the girls were finally asleep and for keeping everything running on the many occasions when I had to just lock into the laptop. Making this happen was one of the biggest challenges I have ever accepted, but this would still just be floating about in my imagination if it wasn't for you holding the fort like you have done. Life with you is the door I will always walk through. You make the mess doable and the magic always accessible. Our birthday month will be just that from now on! The best is yet to come.

yellow
kite

books to help you live a good life

Join the conversation and tell
us how you live a #goodlife